I0885920

PRAISE FOR

FASTER. MESSIER. TOUGHER.

AND BRADLEY AKUBUIRO

In an era of noise, fear, and confusion, this book is a call to higher ground. But the only way to get there is by finding common ground. Bradley offers leaders not just a strategy but a moral compass. His words remind us that conviction still matters, and trust can still be earned.

—REV. JESSE JACKSON SR.
Civil rights icon

Bradley's steadiness under pressure is remarkable—the kind of composure you can't teach. This book reflects the same calm, clear-eyed approach he brings to navigating the most complex communications challenges of our time.

—ROBERT GIBBS
Former White House press secretary; chief communications and public affairs officer, Warner Bros. Discovery

Trust is built slowly and lost instantly. Bradley understands how leaders earn credibility under fire—and how organizations keep it when the world is watching. While there's a trust deficit in American institutions, they should learn from Bradley's insights before they're in crisis.

—HONORABLE PATRICK J. MURPHY
Thirty-second army undersecretary; former US congressman

Bradley Akubuiro has seen firsthand how high the stakes can get, and *Faster, Messier, Tougher* delivers the kind of honest, actionable advice leaders rarely get. Bradley is a clear, essential voice, and this book is a road map for staying grounded when it matters most.

—MICHAEL GONDA
EVP and chief communications officer, Nike

Crisis doesn't build culture—it exposes it. Bradley Akubuiro understands this with a clarity few can match. Drawing on deep experience, this book offers practical, hard-earned wisdom to help leaders safeguard what matters most when the stakes are highest and the future feels uncertain.

—WHITNEY EICHINGER

Chief communications officer, Southwest Airlines

Bradley distills the chaos of the modern communications landscape into a playbook that's sharp, current, and unflinchingly real.

—KATIE HILL

Senior vice president for communications,
National Football League

Part memoir, part master class, Bradley Akubuiro's *Faster, Messier, Tougher* shows leaders how to harness the power of storytelling to turn crises into defining moments. Bradley's deep understanding of how to guide others through uncertainty is evident throughout—it's a brilliant comms and strategy playbook for the perma-crisis era.

—EMILY RAMSHAW

Co-founder and CEO, *The 19th*

"Even with limited power, you can change anything." That's the lesson of Bradley Akubuiro's career and the message of his compelling book, *Faster, Messier, Tougher*. From foreign war zones to the corporate suites of Boeing, Booz Allen Hamilton, and United Technologies, Akubuiro conducts a master class in strategic communications and vivid storytelling. A must-read for every aspiring great communicator.

—CHRIS WHIPPLE

New York Times best-selling author of *The Gatekeepers: How the White House Chiefs of Staff Define Every Presidency* and *Uncharted: How Trump Beat Biden, Harris, and the Odds in the Wildest Campaign in History*

FASTER. MESSIER. TOUGHER.

BRADLEY AKUBUIRO

FASTER. MESSIER. TOUGHER.

CRISIS COMMUNICATION STRATEGIES IN AN AN ERA OF POPULISM, AI, AND DISTRUST

Entrepreneur | Books

Copyright © 2026 by Bradley Akubuiro.

All rights reserved. No part of this book may be used or reproduced in any manner whatsoever without prior written consent of the author, except as provided by the United States of America copyright law.

Published by Entrepreneur® Books, Charleston, South Carolina.
An imprint of Advantage Media Group.

Entrepreneur® Books is a registered trademark of Entrepreneur Media, LLC and used under license to Advantage Media Group.

Printed in the United States of America.

10 9 8 7 6 5 4 3 2 1

ISBN: 979-8-89701-041-7 (Hardcover)
ISBN: 979-8-89701-042-4 (eBook)
ISBN: 979-8-89701-043-1 (Audiobook)

Library of Congress Control Number: Applied

Cover and layout design by Matthew Morse.

This custom publication is intended to provide accurate information and the opinions of the author in regard to the subject matter covered. It is sold with the understanding that the publisher, Entrepreneur® Books, is not engaged in rendering legal, financial, or professional services of any kind. If legal advice or other expert assistance is required, the reader is advised to seek the services of a competent professional.

A note on the stories that follow: Many are drawn from my years at United Technologies (now RTX), Pratt & Whitney, and Boeing. I have recounted them as I experienced them, though memory and perspective are inherently imperfect. Any errors or mischaracterizations are mine alone.

Since 1977, Entrepreneur Media has been dedicated to inspiring, informing, and celebrating the innovators who drive business forward. Entrepreneur® Books, launched in 2024 through a partnership with Entrepreneur Media, continues that mission by helping business and thought leaders share their insights, experiences, and expertise through custom books. Opinions expressed by authors of Entrepreneur® Books are their own. To be considered for publication, please visit books.Entrepreneur.com.

12-03-2025 3:4

To Junior and Samantha—lost too soon.

To Allison—always.

CONTENTS

ABOUT THE AUTHOR

Bradley is a nationally recognized expert on corporate reputation. A partner at Bully Pulpit International, he leads the firm's corporate communications practice and provides change communications, high-visibility crisis management, and media relations counsel to some of the world's most notable brands. Previously, Bradley was the chief spokesperson and head of global media relations for the Boeing Company. Bradley has also led global media relations and public affairs for United Technologies Corporation, now RTX, and served as a management consultant at the firm Booz Allen Hamilton, policy advisor to Rev. Jesse Jackson Sr., and governance reform consultant to the Republic of Liberia following fourteen years of civil war. A nationally recognized expert in his field, Bradley has been quoted by outlets such as *Bloomberg*, *Axios*, and *The Boston Globe*, and his columns have been featured in *Business Insider*, *Forbes*, and *Inc.* magazine, for which he writes a regular column. In 2022, he was included in the 40 Under 40 lists by both *Crain's Chicago Business* and *PRWeek*. He is an adjunct lecturer at the Medill School of Journalism, Media, Integrated Marketing Communications at Northwestern University, where he serves on the board of advisors. He also serves on the boards of the Institute for Public Relations and *The 19th* and is a member of the Accrediting Council on Education in Journalism and Mass Communication. Bradley resides in Chicago with his wife, Allison, also a senior voice in the communications industry. From academia to journalism and from agency leadership to corporate boardrooms, Bradley is driven by a desire to elevate communication as a force for change, resilience, and responsibility.

ACKNOWLEDGMENTS

I am deeply grateful to Allison England, my companion in life and my sharpest thought partner in this project, for her wisdom, love, and the space to wrestle with ideas that matter.

Also to my mother, Darlene, who taught me patience and gave me confidence; to my father, Edmond, who taught me to push for excellence; and to my sisters, Ashley and Sydnee, who have brought me joy and taught me resilience. My family has been my foundation through every chapter of this journey.

At Bully Pulpit International (BPI), my partners and colleagues challenge me daily to push the boundaries of what's possible when business, politics, and culture collide. BPI's mission drives so much of what I do, and this book exists because of the conversations, debates, and breakthroughs we've had together.

Northwestern University and Medill nurtured my belief that great storytelling requires both intellectual rigor and uncompromising integrity. To my colleagues across communications and public affairs, thank you for the late-night strategy sessions, the bold experiments, and the collective push to elevate our craft when it mattered most.

I owe debts to my mentors across every chapter—Rainbow PUSH, Liberia, Booz Allen, United Technologies Corporation, and Boeing—who taught me that voice, purpose, and justice aren't abstract concepts. They're tools for change. Each stop along my journey shaped how I see leadership in moments that count.

To everyone who contributed to this book through insights, edits, challenges, and encouragement: You turned an idea into something real. And to my publisher and editors, thank you for recognizing a voice worth amplifying and a vision worth bringing to life.

FOREWORD

CHARLES WHITAKER
Dean, Medill School of Journalism, Media,
Integrated Marketing Communications
Northwestern University

I first met Bradley Akubuiro when he was an eighteen-year-old freshman at the Medill School. What struck me immediately wasn't just his intellectual curiosity (though that was evident) but his instinctive understanding that journalism and communication were fundamentally about service. Even then, he grasped something many practitioners take years to learn: the power of storytelling to shape not just narratives, but outcomes.

Roughly two decades later, as I watch Bradley lead through some of the most complex communication challenges of our time, I'm reminded that we are living through a moment that demands exactly the kind of principled leadership he embodies—and that this book so urgently prescribes.

The forces reshaping our information ecosystem have arrived faster and with more destructive potential than most anticipated. Social media and the balkanized landscape of information consumption have fractured the concept of shared truth. Algorithms have heightened our tribal instincts, weaponizing our once-shared values, such as an appreciation for diversity and inclusion. Corporate leaders find themselves navigating not just business challenges but also cultural warfare, where every statement becomes a political act and every silence an accusation. From my position leading one of the nation's premier journalism schools, I have a front-row seat on how these forces play out, not only across industry and government but in the academy as well.

This is why communicators can no longer afford to operate from the sidelines. The stakes are too high, the consequences too immediate, and the margin for error too thin. We are being called to lead—not just speak, but lead—through uncertainty that would have been unimaginable when Bradley first entered Northwestern.

I've had the privilege of watching Bradley's evolution from that curious teenager into one of the most trusted voices in corporate communications. As an undergraduate, he didn't just report on the advocacy efforts to free BBC journalist Roxana Saberi, a Medill alumna imprisoned in Iran; he helped organize them from Northwestern's campus, catching the attention of Rev. Jesse Jackson and launching a trajectory that would take him from policy work to Fortune 50 boardrooms. As a professional, he has helped Boeing navigate its most challenging period and helped guide United Technologies Corporation through transformation and complex global crises, and he continues to counsel leaders at some of the top brands domestically and abroad on how to maintain integrity when the world feels like it's coming apart.

What makes Bradley uniquely qualified to write this book isn't just his experience; it's his approach. Throughout his career, he's operated from a core principle that effective communication requires both moral clarity and tactical precision. He understands that in our hyperconnected, hyperpolarized world, reputation isn't just about what you say—it's about whether people trust you enough to believe you when it matters most.

At Medill, we've long believed that great communicators are made, not born. They're forged through rigorous training, real-world testing, and an unwavering commitment to the craft. Bradley exemplifies this journey. From student to practitioner to trusted advisor to educator—he now teaches the next generation in our professional master's program—he's demonstrated that excellence in communication isn't about avoiding difficult conversations but about showing up for them with preparation, purpose, and integrity.

When Bradley asked me to officiate his wedding to Allison, herself a communications powerhouse, I was honored to do so, not just as his former professor but as someone who had watched him become the kind of leader our profession desperately needs. Their partnership reflects the collaborative spirit that defines the best of our field.

This book arrives at a moment when that impact has never been more critical. We are witnessing a crisis of institutional trust that threatens the very foundations of democratic discourse. Corporate leaders who once could rely on carefully crafted statements and traditional media relationships now find themselves in direct conversation with stakeholders who have every tool to fact-check, amplify, or demolish their messages in real time.

Faster, Messier, Tougher isn't just an observation about our current moment; it's a road map for navigating it effectively and with integrity. Bradley doesn't offer easy answers, because there aren't any. Instead, he provides something more valuable: a framework for thinking through complexity, tools for maintaining authenticity under pressure, and examples of what principled leadership looks like when the stakes are highest.

What you'll find in these pages is both practical wisdom and moral argument. Bradley shows us that the choice isn't between being strategic and being authentic; it's finding the courage to be both simultaneously. He demonstrates that in an era of mistrust, transparency isn't just good policy; it's an essential tool for survival. And he makes the case that communicators who retreat to safety are ultimately serving no one.

The world has become faster, messier, and tougher. But as Bradley reminds us throughout this book, these aren't just challenges to endure; they're opportunities for leaders who are willing to step up, speak clearly, and do the hard work of rebuilding trust, one conversation at a time.

For communicators ready to meet this moment, there could be no better guide.

INTRODUCTION

READ THE ROOM OR RISK EVERYTHING

I didn't learn crisis planning in a boardroom. I learned it by walking through the neighborhood. Like so many other young Black men in America, I had lost multiple friends to homicide before I was old enough to get a learner's permit. "Don't get caught slippin'," my friends and I would say. This meant stay alert, understand your surroundings, be clear-eyed about your vulnerabilities, and always have a contingency plan.

In my teenage years, I was constantly assessing risks and preparing options: which streets to walk versus which to avoid, which yards I could cut through if I had to run, which bullies were just scrappers versus those who might pull a gun on you if you tried to fight back.

When I was sixteen, Chris, a childhood friend of mine, was released from prison after a stint for drug dealing. My parents had urged me to stay away from him, but I'd desperately missed his presence in my life. Chris just had this aura about him, a confidence that made you feel invincible simply from being in his presence. He had a way of channeling his charisma that made you feel like you were the only person who mattered.

One night after basketball, Chris suggested we head back to his place. I was hungry, so I told him we had to walk to McDonald's first. As we walked up to his building after our burger run, laughing about how we'd convinced the cashier to let us walk through the drive-through, we heard tires chirping as a car pulled off recklessly from the curb. A few uneasy minutes later, we found out why. Chris's apartment door had been kicked in, and his home was littered with bullet casings. The PlayStation was still on, but his roommate, Stretch, who had been playing it, was a bloody, mangled heap on the couch.

I felt sick. If it hadn't been for our impromptu stop, we'd have ended up in body bags next to Stretch. When I finally snapped out of the shock, my mind began racing through all the variables: Who were all the people who could possibly want Chris or Stretch dead? The shooter had driven past us; had he made out who we were?

The scenarios would inform my every move in the days and weeks to come. I'd throw away the outfit I'd been wearing that night, stay inside as much as possible for the next few weeks, and let friends know not to share my whereabouts with anyone. Above all, I'd avoid Chris. I not only couldn't be seen with him but also couldn't talk to him or acknowledge that I knew him at all.

This foresight came in handy a few weeks later at the local laundromat, where I liked to go for snacks. Someone I hadn't seen before walked in and started staring my way like he was watching me. After a few minutes, he walked up to me and said, "You look like a nigga I know. Nigga named Stretch. You look just like him."

My heart dropped to my stomach. "I don't know him," I said.

"You sure? You look like you could be his cousin."

I knew he was searching my eyes for some sort of reaction, so I turned away as casually as possible. “Nah. Don’t know who that is.”

After another two minutes, which felt like twenty, I bought a soda and chips from the cashier and made my way like I was headed for the bathroom, knowing there was a back exit around the corner. I slipped out, crossed the street, and went into the church next door. For now, I was safe.

As a kid too young to even have a high school diploma, I had become used to making these sorts of calculations on a daily basis. In which scenarios would I try to escape? When would I stand my ground? And when would I need to preemptively strike? If I misjudged a situation, I knew it could cost me my life.

This real-life training in risk assessment, contingency planning, and reading situations would prove invaluable decades later, when I found myself navigating corporate crises at the highest levels. The stakes may be different, but the mindset is identical: Understand your environment, know your vulnerabilities, and always have an exit strategy.

What surprised me when I entered the corporate world was how few people in business actually understood and applied these basic principles.

MY CRISIS COMMUNICATIONS EDUCATION

I moved several times growing up, but no matter where my family landed, the us-versus-them divide was always apparent to me. Whether I was in Pittsburgh, Atlanta, or Springfield, Massachusetts, I couldn’t help but see how vastly different the Black and Latino parts of town were from the white suburbs just a few miles away. It wasn’t until

I became a student at Northwestern University (NU) that I truly learned how to harness the power of communication, and authentic storytelling, to bridge this divide.

As a student facing financial pressure that nearly forced me to leave school, I found myself at the center of a campus-wide conversation about diversity and access. It was 2008, and only eighty-seven Black freshmen had enrolled at Northwestern out of a class of 2,078, dropping Black student enrollment to its lowest point since 1972. I was leading the NU Ambassadors, Northwestern's undergraduate admissions program focused on recruiting more Black and Latino students, and we had a crisis on our hands.

I built an unlikely coalition between frustrated students and the administrators they blamed by convincing student leaders to turn what would have been a protest against the administration into a rally to build support for change. It became a shared mission. We built recruitment programs, and we created momentum around them with record levels of student participation. And I talked to anyone who would listen about not only what we were building but also where the support system fell short. I spoke to *The Daily Northwestern*, *Northwestern Magazine*, and the university's student broadcast network. I used my own imperfect experience to ground my message.

Real results followed. By the end of my four years, the enrollment of Black students at Northwestern had increased by 22 percent. Latino student enrollment was up more than 50 percent. Obviously my work was only one component, but it was the first public affairs campaign I'd ever been a leader in. The experience encapsulated all the components necessary to drive transformation: speed, clarity, credibility, coalition building, and a compelling story. And being central to such a successful change effort as a college student provided a valuable lesson. Even with limited power, you can change anything, as long as you have a clear sense of purpose and a structured approach. It's a lesson I have carried with me throughout my career.

BOARDROOMS, BACK CHANNELS, AND BACKLASH

From Northwestern, my path toured me through a series of experiences that would shape my understanding of what it means to effect clear and vital communications under pressure. I served as a policy advisor to Rev. Jesse Jackson Sr., where I learned the power of symbolism and collective action and how opportunities for the greatest change often present themselves during moments of crisis. Working with Rev. Jackson taught me that authentic leadership requires finding the intersection between moral clarity and tailored communication, especially when the stakes are highest.

Later, I found myself in Liberia, working as a governance reform consultant to help rebuild a functioning democracy after fourteen years of civil war. Six weeks into my time on the ground, I was working with cabinet-level ministers and legislative leaders to coordinate the establishment of a national leadership development program and policy for the country which had lost substantial institutional capacity.

As one government report noted, "While roads and buildings can be rebuilt, if the national psyche is not rebuilt and rooted on sound foundation, focusing on personal development, character building and good ethics—in five years, Liberia will be right back to square one."[1] My experience working for and learning from giants like President Ellen Johnson Sirleaf and Amos Sawyer solidified my belief in the power of vision and how, when aspirational words were

1 Internal memo to the Liberian president from the Liberian Governance Commission.

combined with bold actions, they can help reestablish trust even in the direst of circumstances.

The corporate world followed, from working as a management consultant at Booz Allen Hamilton to leading communications for military jet engine programs at Pratt & Whitney to running global media and public affairs communications for the $77 billion United Technologies Corporation (UTC). During my time at UTC, I ended up facing an unexpected and extremely high-stakes situation (detailed in chapter 2 of this book) that turned everything I thought I knew about crisis communications upside down. Then came Boeing, which brought even bigger challenges. As chief spokesperson, I represented the company through the aftermath of the 737 MAX crisis, COVID-19, and the national conversation around race following the murder of George Floyd.

Each step in my career deepened my understanding of how geopolitics, business strategy, and communication collide in real time, often with thousands of jobs and billions of dollars hanging in the balance. Now, I have the honor of bringing all these different experiences together as an advisor to boards and corporate leaders on reputation management in this perma-crisis era. My role as a partner at Bully Pulpit International, an advisory firm founded by leaders of the Obama campaigns and administration, has involved work with the National Football League (NFL), McDonald's, Boeing, Hyatt, and Levi Strauss, as well as some of the world's biggest brands across finance, healthcare, sports, tech, philanthropy, and higher education.

My goal in writing this book is to share the lessons I've learned on my journey from the neighborhood to the executive suites of some of the biggest corporations in the world with you. In particular, I hope that I succeed in championing the idea that trust is the cornerstone of successful communications before, during, and after a crisis. And trust begins with authenticity.

A WORD ABOUT THE AUTHENTICITY PARADOX

Before continuing with the role of authenticity in corporate communications, I would like to address the elephant in the room that every minority leader in your organization knows is there. I first wrote about the authenticity paradox in my *Forbes* article, "The Catch-22 of Authenticity for Minority Leaders."[2] Being authentic as a minority leader has always felt like a high-wire act: You're balancing genuine representation of your community with remaining effective within broader corporate structures. But that challenge has intensified dramatically as figures such as Elon Musk push slogans like "DEI must DIE," and both he and President Trump routinely blame diversity, equity, and inclusion (DEI) initiatives for corporate shortcomings and safety failures.

In this reality, a subset of people in your organization don't just feel disempowered; they feel like political pawns. What we're witnessing isn't purely cultural. But the injection of identity politics into previously neutral corporate territory has pushed both individuals and institutions onto contested ground where every decision, from supply chains to hiring practices, carries political weight that didn't exist a decade ago.

How leaders address this shift will impact both macro and micro scales for years to come. It's not just about managing a workforce

---

2 Bradley Akubuiro, "The Catch-22 of Authenticity for Minority Leaders," *Forbes*, October 4, 2021, https://www.forbes.com/councils/forbescommunicationscouncil/2021/10/04/the-catch-22-of-authenticity-for-minority-leaders/.

anymore; it's about navigating a landscape where business decisions have become inseparable from cultural and political positioning.

This isn't just professional for me. It's deeply personal.

But for anyone with even a passing interest in this space, it's critical to recognize that we are at an inflection point. When the rules change this fundamentally, anyone and everyone who built their career on the old playbook will need to start over.

THE OLD PLAYBOOK IS DEAD: HERE'S WHAT'S NEXT

For all of us in crisis communications, it feels like the world shifted beneath our feet while we weren't looking. The strategies that served us for decades—the careful statements, the measured responses, the wait-and-see approaches—are more than just ineffective; they're actively dangerous.

The speed problem: When I started in this industry, you had hours, sometimes days, to craft the perfect response. Today, silence for thirty minutes gets interpreted as guilt, indifference, or incompetence. The old playbook's emphasis on deliberation and legal review now reads as tone-deaf delay.

The trust problem: Traditional media gatekeepers who once helped to separate signal from noise are gone. Institutions that used to provide some measure of objective truth, such as newsrooms, fact-checkers, and even platform moderators, have been eliminated or compromised. We're operating in a landscape where half-truths travel faster than facts, and your corporate statement competes directly with conspiracy theories for audience attention (if that statement even reaches your audience at all).

The polarization problem: The old playbook assumed you could craft a message that would satisfy most reasonable people. That middle ground has been obliterated. Corporate positions on everything from diversity initiatives to trade policy are now filtered through political tribes. Neutrality isn't just impossible; it's seen as cowardice by all sides.

The personalization problem: CEOs once spoke to "stakeholders" and "the public." Now, they're speaking to micro-audiences who filter every message through the lens of "my people, my party, and me." The broad-appeal communications strategies of the past can't navigate this new hierarchy of relevance.

The weaponization problem: Perhaps most dangerously, the old playbook's emphasis on defensive posturing and liability protection has made companies sitting ducks for bad actors and opponents who understand how to exploit corporate communication patterns. They know you'll be slow, cautious, and desperate to appear reasonable, and they'll use every one of those instincts against you.

WHAT THIS BOOK DELIVERS

This book isn't just another crisis communication manual filled with the same tired advice about "getting ahead of the story." This is a field guide to help you successfully navigate a fundamentally changed landscape.

The uncomfortable truth is that many organizations clinging to the old playbook aren't just failing; they're making their exposure worse. The reason I wrote *Faster, Messier, Tougher: Crisis Communication Strategies in an Era of Populism, AI, and Distrust* is to offer a new framework for a world where corporate communication and crisis communication have become indistinguishable and where the ability to navigate perpetual controversy isn't just a nice-to-have skill; it's essential.

The scenario planning I learned as a teenager (understanding your environment, assessing threats, and having contingency plans) goes beyond survival instinct. It's now a core competency for anyone responsible for protecting an organization's reputation in the current moment. The only difference is that instead of street gangs, corporate leaders must navigate misinformation campaigns, cultural warfare, and technological disruptions that can destroy decades of trust-building in minutes.

Whether you're a CEO, head of communications, or otherwise responsible for protecting an organization's reputation, this book is your road map to not just surviving the storm but emerging from its wake stronger than ever.

PART ONE

REWRITING THE RULES OF ENGAGEMENT

CHAPTER ONE

FROM THE AGE OF IMPACT TO THE AGE OF ISSUES

In the early 2020s, the consensus among highly paid corporate communications consultants was that companies, and particularly high-profile CEOs, should take definitive stands on thorny societal issues. The prevailing view was that, as trust in government leadership waned, people were now looking to private sector executives to pick up the mantle of societal leadership. People in roles similar to mine encouraged companies to weigh in on social conversations in the media, post core value statements on their websites, and fund cause-oriented philanthropic and advocacy efforts through earmarked foundations and charitable contributions. Employee engagement became a cornerstone of corporate culture as employee experience came to rival customer experience. Company leaders were warned that the world had changed and so had their roles, and that "statesmanship" was now part of the job description.

Recognizing that something truly unprecedented was happening in companies across America, I began writing a column for *Inc.*, focusing on the intersection of corporate culture and values. I called it "The Age of Impact." There was no way for me to know then just how short-lived that remarkable age would be.

THE RISE AND FALL OF THE AGE OF IMPACT

Every so often, an event so transformative comes along that it splits time in two: before and after. The Declaration of Independence. The Emancipation Proclamation. The Great Depression. World War II. The Civil Rights Movement. The 9/11 attack. These weren't just major events; they were turning points that changed both how America saw itself and how it operated. There's no debate that the COVID-19 pandemic belongs on that list. What began as a global health emergency quickly became something bigger: a reckoning with how we live, how we work, who we trust. And what kind of future we're really prepared for. The pandemic disrupted life and exposed the fault lines we'd been ignoring and accelerated shifts we still haven't come to terms with. We're living in the aftermath now.

The World Health Organization officially declared that COVID-19 had become a worldwide pandemic on March 11, 2020. Two days later, the United States followed suit.[3]

With government restrictions on travel and the imposition of national and state-specific public health guidelines, including recommendations for social distancing, prohibitions on large public gatherings, school closures, mask mandates, and stay-at-home orders, many felt like the world had come to a screeching halt. Many nonessential workers were furloughed or laid off. Others, particularly those in

---

3 David J. Sencer CDC Museum, "CDC Museum COVID-19 Timeline," Centers for Disease Control and Prevention, accessed September 7, 2025, https://www.cdc.gov/museum/timeline/covid19.html.

white-collar professions, were encouraged—if not required—to work from home.

A revolution in how Americans experience work took hold.

For many, working from home came with a remarkable set of benefits, including being able to nix long commutes. For the first time, it was possible to hold down a great-paying job while also being present for family and personal pursuits. People realized that they could give equal time to work and their personal lives while still meeting both their professional and individual responsibilities. No longer limited by the need to be close to a company's offices, remote white-collar employees could seek out lateral moves and opportunities for promotion without having to relocate. If you didn't like your boss or wanted more money than your current company was willing or able to pay, you could simply apply for another position anywhere in the country with little restriction. And the competition for talent was fierce. I personally had employees leave jobs at my company for lateral positions that paid 50 to 60 percent more out of the gate.

The ball was in these workers' courts, and they took this power and ran with it. Some termed this a great migration. Employees switched jobs like they were changing outfits—always open to finding out if another organization might provide a better fit. Employers, in fierce competition to hire and retain the best and the brightest, started exploring ways to go beyond financial incentives to offer the psychological security that comes with a sense of belonging to a distinct culture and community.

Blue-collar workers wouldn't be left behind for long. Joe Biden's election to the presidency in November 2020 ushered in one of the most pro-union eras in contemporary political history.[4] This pro-labor orientation emboldened workers across diverse sectors to pursue unionization, from Apple Store employees in Oklahoma City to Trader Joe's workers in Massachusetts.

On the heels of the pandemic, America seemed to reconnect with its benevolent side. Companies, foundations, and individuals donated a whopping $557 billion in 2023,[5] a remarkable number given the elevated cost of living and nonstop headlines warning of an impending, although never materializing, recession. American culture was embracing impact in new and meaningful ways. Yet even as America was embracing this spirit of collective generosity, the country was about to confront its deepest wounds.

A Reckoning Regarding Race

Two months into the pandemic, on May 25, 2020, white Minneapolis police officer Derek Michael Chauvin threw George Floyd, a Black man, onto the ground, kneeling on his neck for over nine minutes as Floyd fought for his life, crying out, "I can't breathe." The incident was caught on video by a teenaged bystander and quickly went viral, with over 1.4 billion views on Twitter alone in just twelve days.[6] Floyd's murder happened just weeks after the tragic March

4 Eyal Press, "Biden Is the Most Pro-Labor President Since F.D.R. Will It Matter in November?" *New Yorker*, April 18, 2024, https://www.newyorker.com/news/daily-comment/biden-is-the-most-pro-labor-president-since-fdr-will-it-matter-in-november.

5 "Giving USA: U.S. Charitable Giving Totaled $557.16 Billion in 2023," Lilly Family School of Philanthropy, June 25, 2024, https://philanthropy.indianapolis.iu.edu/news-events/news/_news/2024/giving-usa-us-charitable-giving-totaled-557.16-billion-in-2023.html.

6 Sam Blake, "George Floyd Protest Videos Were Watched over 1.4 Billion Times in the First 12 Days of Unrest," *dot.LA*, June 20, 2020, https://dot.la/george-floyd-video-2646171522.html.

2020 shooting death of twenty-six-year-old Breonna Taylor, a Black woman whose home was mistakenly invaded by Louisville police executing a no-knock search warrant for a different address.

These incidents not only fueled an already-established Black Lives Matter (BLM) movement but also sparked meaningful conversations about race in boardrooms throughout the country. Solving generations of systemic inequity became a priority for many organizations, and diversity, equity, and inclusion (DEI) became a major touchpoint in corporate America, evidenced by the fact that chief diversity officer became the C-suite's fastest-growing title.[7] Employers raced to show their DEI bona fides, issuing reports proclaiming their commitment to racial equity in the workplace.

By every indication, the country was swept up in a collective chorus of kumbayas. That is, until it wasn't.

According to Isaac Newton's third law of motion, every action has an equal and opposite reaction. In my experience, that law applies as much to human nature as it does to the laws of physics, and it appeared to be playing out in American life as the momentum that propelled the age of impact began to slow, stop, and then shift into reverse. By the middle of 2023, the political polarization that would come to define the 2024 presidential election cycle and beyond was gaining steam. It was becoming clear that the pendulum was swinging away from the flexible work and the impact and inclusion policies of the pandemic era to the "my people, my party, and me" point of view of those who disagreed, many of whom had come to feel left out, dismissed, or downright discriminated against themselves as a result.

---

7 Mita Mallick, "What's Next for Chief Diversity Officers?," *Fast Company*, October 16, 2023, https://www.fastcompany.com/90967182/whats-next-for-chief-diversity-officers.

For corporate leaders, taking a stand was becoming risky business. What followed would demonstrate exactly why.

A BURGEONING BACKLASH

By 2023, the robust job market had slowed considerably, and the newfound power flexing of employees and job seekers declined with it. Participants in the great migration now found themselves with pocketed resumes and looming layoffs. As the job market cooled,[8] employers began examining the cost–benefit of working from home as they sought a return to pre-pandemic levels of productivity and bemoaned the waste of empty offices they were still paying for. The return-to-office movement began to take hold.

At the same time, employers began pushing back publicly and forcefully against the burgeoning labor movements of the last few years, using their considerable political weight and financial resources to thwart, stall, or at least suck the power out of nascent unionizing efforts.

In recent years, for example, major corporations, from Apple to Chipotle, have faced costly strikes when management implemented new workplace policies, compensation changes, or disciplinary measures without adequately consulting with newly organized workers, leading to tens of thousands of employees walking off the job and accusing management of a blatant disregard for collective bargaining processes. Examples extend

8 Victor Huang and En Ping Cheng, "Job Openings and Hires Decline in 2023 as the Labor Market Cools," *Monthly Labor Review*, U.S. Bureau of Labor Statistics, September 2024, https://www.bls.gov/opub/mlr/2024/article/job-openings-and-hires-decline-in-2023.htm.

across aerospace, tech, food and beverage, telecom, and beyond.[9] From the employer's perspective, the message was clear. Labor was out. Management was, once again, in.

By 2024, fewer people were giving money to charity compared to previous years. As the number of people giving less than $500 a year, who make up the vast majority of philanthropic givers, dropped significantly, large donors attempted to pick up the slack. According to experts, this trend of fewer donors giving more is not sustainable and indicates a widening gap between generosity and participation. There's a growing fear among those in the nonprofit sector that this gap in giving could put many charities on dangerous financial ground.

Perhaps the most far-reaching backlash to the age of impact has been the dismantling of the DEI movement. DEI opponents began

---

9 "17,000 AT&T Workers Across the Southeast Strike over Contract Negotiations," WBAA (NPR Member Station), August 18, 2024, https://www.wbaa.org/2024-08-17/17000-att-workers-across-the-southeast-strike-over-contract-negotiations; "17,000 Workers at AT&T Southeast Strike over Unfair Labor Practices," Communications Workers of America, August 16, 2024, https://cwa-union.org/news/releases/17000-workers-att-southeast-strike-over-unfair-labor-practices; "AT&T Southeast Workers End Month-Long Strike," Labor Notes, September 19, 2024, https://labornotes.org/blogs/2024/09/att-southeast-workers-end-month-long-strike; "Boeing Shares Fall 2.7% After Workers Reject Latest Labor Offer," Reuters, October 24, 2024, https://www.reuters.com/business/aerospace-defense/boeing-shares-fall-27-after-workers-reject-latest-labor-offer-2024-10-24/; "Boeing Factory Strike Ends as Workers Vote to Accept Contract," MPR News (NPR Member Station), November 5, 2024, https://www.mprnews.org/story/2024/11/05/boeing-factory-strike-ends-as-workers-vote-to-accept-contract; "Chipotle Illegally Denied Raises to Unionized Workers, Labor Watchdog Says," CBS News, August 26, 2024, https://www.cbsnews.com/news/chipotle-denied-raises-to-unionized-workers-nlrb/; "Chipotle May Have Violated Workers' Unionization Rights, US Labor Board Says," Associated Press, August 27, 2024, https://apnews.com/article/chipotle-niccol-starbucks-teamsters-nlrb-ec29fd4f727572ee1cc3b2f834084f9d; "After Two Years Without a Contract, Unionized Chipotle Workers Call for Nationwide Boycott," Labor Union News, December 4, 2024, https://www.laborunionnews.com/2024/12/04/after-two-years-without-a-contract-unionized-chipotle-workers-call-for-nationwide-boycott/; "Apple Retail Union-CWA Local 6016 Members Secured a Tentative Labor Agreement with Apple," Communications Workers of America, September 12, 2024, https://cwa-union.org/news/e-newsletter/2024-09-12.

using every mechanism at their disposal to turn back the clock. At the state level, power players such as conservative Florida Governor Ron DeSantis, backed by like-minded legislators, flexed their political might to punish any institutions that promoted a so-called "woke" agenda. In 2022, DeSantis-appointed trustees famously fired the president of New College of Florida, a liberal arts honors college known for its academic excellence and unabashed support of the LGBTQ community. Soon thereafter, the college's new right-leaning board and administration eliminated the college's DEI office and banned the use of personal pronouns in email signatures. That same year, DeSantis orchestrated the removal of major Florida employer Walt Disney World's tax-exempt status after the company publicly opposed his Parental Rights in Education Act, commonly referred to as the "don't say gay" law, which restricts discussions of LGBTQ topics in academic settings.

But the most significant rollback occurred on the national stage with the 2023 Supreme Court decision in *Students for Fair Admissions v. President and Fellows of Harvard College*,[10] which sounded a death knell for affirmative action in both the public and private arenas. Although the ruling was specific to affirmative action in higher-education admissions, it served to embolden DEI opponents across the board. Then, in January 2025, in the first two days of his second term, President Trump signed two executive orders eliminating DEI programs throughout the federal government and removing nondiscrimination as a criterion for being awarded a federal contract.[11] In response, many in boardrooms have felt compelled to reassess and,

10 *Students for Fair Admissions, Inc. v. President and Fellows of Harvard College*, 600 U.S. 181, 143 S. Ct. 2141 (2023).

11 Exec. Order No. 14173, *Ending Illegal Discrimination and Restoring Merit-Based Opportunity*, 90 Fed. Reg. 8633 (January 21, 2025), https://www.federalregister.gov/d/2025-02097.

at the very least, rebrand—if not eliminate—their DEI initiatives, or risk significant legal ramifications.

While many major companies, including Harley-Davidson and John Deere, decided to roll back their DEI initiatives, perhaps no company has felt the boomerang effects of this rapidly changing landscape more than Target.

In 2022 and 2023, right-wing advocacy groups called for a boycott of Target because it was displaying and selling merchandise supporting LGBTQ Pride Month.[12] Several Target stores received threats, and there were reports that employees had experienced harassment. In response, the company pulled some of this merchandise from select store shelves. This, in turn, prompted a boycott by LGBTQ supporters who were opposed to Target's giving in to conservative pressure.

Then, in January 2025, on the heels of the president's anti-DEI executive orders and citing political pressures and shifting public attitudes, Target Corporation announced that it was eliminating its robust DEI initiatives,[13] including its Racial Equity Action and Change program, which had pledged over $2 billion to support minority-owned businesses. In response, civil rights groups organized boycotts, and shareholders filed a suit, claiming that ending its DEI programs damaged stock values. Target's sales declined significantly in the weeks following its decision to turn its back on DEI.[14]

---

12 Gloria Oladipo, "Right-Wing Group Takes Aim at Target for Offering Pride-Themed Merchandise," *Guardian*, May 25, 2023, https://www.theguardian.com/world/2023/may/25/cpac-target-removes-pride-merchandise.

13 Siddharth Cavale, "Target Ending DEI Initiatives amid Trump's Order on Diversity Programs," Reuters, January 25, 2025, https://www.reuters.com/business/retail-consumer/target-ends-its-3-year-diversity-equity-inclusion-initiatives-2025-01-24.

14 James Rogers, "Tariff Uncertainty, DEI Backlash Hurt Target's Results. Price Increases Are 'the Very Last Resort,' CEO Says," *MarketWatch*, May 21, 2025, https://www.marketwatch.com/story/targets-stock-drops-as-earnings-fall-below-forecasts-and-the-outlook-was-lowered-5e3012a3.

In just a few short years, we'd gone from the age of impact to the age of issues, where change is the only constant, and crisis communications has become synonymous with corporate communications. Navigating this damned-if-you-do-and-damned-if-you-don't world requires a new strategy.

Consider this book your guide.

CRISIS COMMUNICATIONS IN THE AGE OF ISSUES

Traditional media is dying by the day, and the elimination of fact-checkers on social media platforms means there is literally nobody empowered to defend the truth. From a communications standpoint, we have to accept the fact that we now operate in a society of half-truths, where large swaths of the population will latch onto tiny kernels of veracity wrapped in layers of lies and webs of confusion. You, me, and the companies we represent have only ourselves to rely on when it comes to protecting our reputations and interests. As comms pros, we are tasked with the impossible job of shielding our stakeholders from all the misinformation, disinformation, half-truths, and all-out intentional lies that can and will spread at the speed of light. No one is coming to save us.

As a business or comms leader reading this, I can't blame you for wanting to run or, at the very least, put your head in the sand hoping this chaos will somehow be replaced by a new era, perhaps one that resembles an age of reason.

Stop. Take a deep breath. We can get through this.

You picked up this book because you are ready to face whatever challenges come your way head-on. Sure, the present feels grim, and the future seems daunting, but that's why you're here—to acquire the tools you'll need to see your organization (and your career) through the dumpster fire that is the current state of crisis communications. But remember, this is where we thrive. We're the folks who see a fire and run toward the flames.

And we're the ones who have the capacity to find the silver lining in any cloud and the flexibility to pivot on a dime. Despite the uncertainties and the chaos, you have more latitude to leverage communications to achieve your objectives than you might think. It's times like these that set the stage for real impact.

In my experience, organizations are most malleable in moments of crisis and uncertainty. So, invoking the wisdom of Winston Churchill, this is no time to let a good crisis go to waste.

I'm not saying that it's going to be easy. You're going to have to move faster to keep up with unpredictable messages. And you're going to have to get your hands dirty. You'll find yourself punching it out with hostile audiences or taking stands that you know from the outset are going to be unpopular with a certain percentage of the population. Making the sausage is never pretty, but the alternative is to become mincemeat at the hands of those who would do you and your brand harm.

You and your fellow corporate executives will have to toughen up. We all know that when it comes to criticism, C-suite types are notorious for having thin skin and glass jaws. That ends now. You and your organization *will* take hits, so it's time to learn to take a punch if you have any intention of staying in the fight. This moment will require you to change the way you think about reputation, and that includes changing your approach to protecting your brand. It will mean undergoing a crisis communications reeducation of sorts. How do I know? Because I was forced to undergo a transformation of my own, born out of the events in Charlottesville, Virginia, in the summer of 2017.

CHAPTER TWO

MY CRISIS COMMS REEDUCATION

By August of 2017, I considered myself an experienced crisis communicator. I'd dealt with plane crashes and civil wars. Like most professionals, I can point to several experiences in my career that shaped the way I see the world, and as a result, the way I approach my job.

While working for Rev. Jesse Jackson, I learned the power of symbolism and collective action and how often opportunities for the greatest change present themselves during moments of crisis. My work in post–civil war Liberia, helping to rebuild a functioning democracy, solidified my belief in the power of aspirational words from an inspirational leader and how those words, when combined with bold actions, can help reestablish trust even in the direst of circumstances. And as a consultant working on the rollout of the Affordable Care Act, I saw that having a clear vision and an audacious goal can help weather even the most public setbacks.

After my career transition to the corporate world, I came to further understand the power of communications in enacting change. I saw how guiding a major player in aerospace manufacturing to transcend tragedy helped rebuild the company's reputation, paving the way for its continued contributions to the vital work of keeping America's defenses strong.

And no matter the issue, no matter the crisis, I learned that I could count on results as long as I followed a simple playbook: (1) Identify the problem as quickly as possible; (2) determine how to stem the bleeding, a.k.a. containing the situation; (3) communicate clearly to stakeholders the concrete steps you are taking to not only fix the problem but also ensure that the problem won't happen again; and (4) highlight evidence of progress to reinforce that the situation is under control and that the problem is no longer one to worry about.

I felt confident that I had finally reached the point in my career where I could say that I had a solid handle on my craft. And maybe I did. But then Charlottesville happened. And practically overnight, the entire communications operating system I'd spent my career navigating to great success suddenly and without warning flipped on its head.

THE FOUR DAYS THAT CHANGED IT ALL

In the summer of 2017, white nationalists joined forces with other far-right organizations to rally in Charlottesville, Virginia, in protest of the planned removal of a statue of Confederate General Robert E. Lee. On the evening of August 11, the Unite the Right protesters marched with lit torches through the University of Virginia campus, chanting racist and anti-Semitic refrains. This display of racial vitriol was a precursor to the main rally scheduled for the following day in the newly named Emancipation Park (formerly known as Lee Park to honor the infamous leader of the Confederate Army). The estimated five hundred white nationalist demonstrators attending the rally on August 12 were met by one thousand counter-protesters.[15]

Saturday, August 12, 2017

The far-right rally and counter-protests were in full swing when self-proclaimed white supremacist James Alex Fields Jr. deliberately drove his car into the crowd of counter-protesters, killing thirty-two-year-old Heather Heyer and injuring thirty-five others.

In the hours following the attack, the forty-fifth president of the United States, Donald Trump, offered a statement from his golf club in Bedminster, New Jersey: "We condemn in the strongest possible terms this egregious display of hatred, bigotry and violence on many sides, on many sides."[16]

On many sides …

To most of us who had watched scenes of the murder caught on video—a peaceful counter-protest interrupted by screams and people's bodies being hurled through the air—what transpired felt like an open-and-shut case of right versus wrong. The neo-Nazis and white supremacists, who brazenly carried torches, chanted racist and anti-Semitic slogans, and openly patrolled the Charlottesville streets in heavily armed packs with little to no intervention from local police, were the ones who were displaying hatred and bigotry and promoting violence. And one of their followers had killed a woman and injured dozens. It was hard to find room for the president's nuances. For most people, there are no nuances to wanton murder.

---

15 International Association of Chiefs of Police, *Virginia's Response to the Unite the Right Rally*, December 2017, https://www.pshs.virginia.gov/media/governorvirginiagov/secretary-of-public-safety-and-homeland-security/pdf/iacp-after-action-review.pdf.

16 Donald J. Trump, "Remarks: Donald Trump Signs Veterans Act, Addresses Charlottesville—August 12, 2017," *Roll Call*, August 12, 2017, https://rollcall.com/factbase/trump/transcript/donald-trump-remarks-veterans-act-charlottesville-august-12-2017.

Immediately following the president's remarks, the media lit up, and the Twitterverse erupted in a frenzy. People were demanding answers, while the president's defenders scrambled to clarify and water down his comments.

At the time, I was working at United Technologies Corporation (UTC), a then roughly $60 billion global conglomerate of aerospace and building systems companies based outside Hartford, Connecticut. I'd started the job almost exactly a year before. It was one I'd been advocating for and pursuing for two years. It was truly a dream come true, a newly created position at corporate, leading public affairs communications for the enterprise. I was not only based in Washington, DC, but in a spacious office overlooking Pennsylvania Avenue, just a few short blocks from the White House. This role made me the company's chief Washington spokesperson and the head of communications for all things related to politics and policy.

When the job was good, it was amazing, but that week, I felt like I was strapped into the passenger seat of a car in the middle of a slow-motion crash. Greg Hayes, CEO of UTC, was a member of the American Manufacturing Council, a group of prominent chief executives set up to advise President Trump on domestic manufacturing initiatives. From the time the chaos had spilled over in Charlottesville, I'd been trying to weigh the virtue of issuing a statement to distance Greg and the company from the president's remarks.

As a Black man and as an American, the situation made my skin crawl. I wanted to scream from the rooftops that this was a textbook hate crime and that the blame was squarely on one side, not many. But in my role as a spokesperson for UTC, a company that received roughly one-quarter of its revenue from the US government, I knew a higher degree of restraint was required.

What would be the repercussions of a statement that produced even the perception of admonishing the commander-in-chief, particularly one that could be seen as critical of a president known for the premium he put on loyalty?

It was Saturday. No need to rush to an answer over the weekend, I thought. Better to monitor the situation and take stock on Monday.

Monday, August 14, 2017

When Monday finally rolled around, the day's events hit me in the face like a sack of bricks. That morning, Ken Frazier, then the head of Merck & Co. and one of the nation's most prominent Black CEOs, resigned publicly from the American Manufacturing Council, saying, "As a matter of personal conscience, I feel a responsibility to take a stand against intolerance and extremism." He later added that "America's leaders must honor our fundamental values by clearly rejecting expressions of hatred, bigotry, and group supremacy, which run counter to the American ideal that all people are created equal."[17]

BOOM. That was one hell of a statement.

There had always been an unwritten but almost universally followed rule of business that corporate leaders do all that they can to avoid getting caught up in the controversial swirl of politics. For years, business advisory councils were, for practical purposes, pro forma; something government leaders organized to show they were engaging with those who held the levers of the US economy and something business leaders participated in to show employees and shareholders that they were advocating for their interests with those who led the govern-

---

17 Bill Chappell, "CEOs of Merck, Under Armour and Intel Resign from Trump's Business Council," NPR, August 14, 2017, https://www.npr.org/sections/thetwo-way/2017/08/14/543384974/merck-ceo-resigns-from-a-trump-business-council-citing-his-conscience.

ment. Until now, participating in an organization such as the American Manufacturing Council was considered low risk and all prestige and civility. But Ken Frazier had just changed the rules. With zero warning, a prominent CEO had dropped a bombshell on the business community.

In the hours following the Frazier announcement, three more CEOs resigned from government-sponsored industry advisory groups: Kevin Plank of Under Armour, who said his company "engages in innovation and sports, not politics";[18] Brian Krzanich of Intel, who said he was stepping down to "call attention to the serious harm our divided political climate is causing to critical issues";[19] and Scott Paul of the Alliance for American Manufacturing, who tweeted, "I'm resigning from the Manufacturing Jobs Initiative because it's the right thing for me to do."[20]

Maureen Fitzgerald, my colleague who led corporate media relations for UTC, sent a rundown of media requests to a small group that included me; our mutual boss, Chief Communications Officer (CCO) Nancy Lintner; and a few others. We'd received twenty-three inquiries from outlets ranging from CNN and *The New York Times* to *The Daily Beast*. They all wanted to know two things:

1. Our reaction to the Merck CEO resigning from the Manufacturing Council following the president's comments
2. Whether Greg Hayes would continue to serve on the council

---

18 Kevin Plank, "Kevin Plank, Under Armour Founder and CEO Statement," Under Armour Newsroom, August 14, 2017, https://investor.underarmour.com/news-releases/news-release-details/kevin-plank-under-armour-founder-and-ceo-statement.

19 Brian Krzanich, "Intel CEO Leaves American Manufacturing Council," Intel Newsroom, August 14, 2017, https://community.intel.com/t5/Blogs/Intel/Policy-Intel/Intel-CEO-leaves-American-Manufacturing-Council/post/1332986.

20 Scott Paul (@ScottPaulAAM), "I'm resigning from the Manufacturing Jobs Initiative because it's the right thing for me to do," X (formerly Twitter), August 15, 2017, 3:37 p.m., https://twitter.com/scottpaulaam/status/897482381275283456.

The pressure was on, but by the end of the day that Monday, UTC still hadn't broken its silence. A couple of developments during the previous hours had made the decision to hold off easier. For one, following the intense public criticism, Trump had made a second attempt at putting the matter to bed by making a televised announcement from the White House. At 12:38 p.m., the president had been forceful in his condemnation of the perpetrator, saying, "Racism is evil. And those who cause violence in its name are criminals and thugs, including the KKK, neo-Nazis, white supremacists, and other hate groups that are repugnant to everything we hold dear as Americans."[21]

And following that, at 3:20 p.m., Andrew Liveris, CEO of the Dow Chemical Company, who headed up the American Manufacturing Council, issued a statement on behalf of the council. The statement read,

> *As the leaders of companies that have volunteered to contribute to the administration's Manufacturing Jobs Initiative, we condemn the violence this weekend in Charlottesville, Virginia. In the companies we lead, there is no room for hatred, racism, or bigotry. Our thoughts and prayers are with the families who lost loved ones this past weekend and with the people of Virginia. We will continue our work to strengthen the social and economic fabric of communities across the country by creating employment opportunities in manufacturing and rebuilding our workforce.*[22]

---

21 Trump, "Remarks."

22 Andrew Liveris, "Factbox—Trump's Manufacturing Panel CEOs, Companies Comment on Charlottesville," Reuters, August 15, 2017, https://www.reuters.com/article/virginia-protests-merck-co-council-factb/factbox-trumps-manufacturing-panel-ceos-companies-comment-on-charlottesville-idINKCN1AU2IU.

It was following the release of this statement that I told members of the UTC leadership team, "Unless the situation evolves, we should probably sit this one out and continue with our current approach of nonresponse to incoming on the topic."

The next day, I found myself eating those words.

Tuesday, August 15, 2017

Early Tuesday morning, the president poured fresh fuel on the flames with a passionate tweet. "For every CEO who drops out of the Manufacturing Council, I have many to take their place. Grandstanders should not have gone on. JOBS!"[23]

Following that tweet, I spent the rest of the morning tethered to my phone as I attempted to find some internal alignment. I spoke with media relations about their receipt of twenty-five new top-tier media inquiries. I had a call with the heads of HR and diversity and inclusion to talk through the employee response and our DEI posture, one with government relations to discuss the implications of a statement on our political relationships, and still another with legal to talk through our exposure. I also reached out to those monitoring our social media to get a sense of how much volume the conversation had among the public and whether UTC was being called out specifically.

I asked for input from all of these groups as I worked to create a draft statement we could have in our back pocket if and when we needed it. It was starting to become clear that, beyond the inquiries from the media, droves of employees and a number of outside advocacy groups were pushing us to provide a response. I figured it might not be

23 Donald J. Trump, "For every CEO that drops out of the Manufacturing Council, I have many to take their place. Grandstanders should not ... !" X (formerly Twitter), August 15, 2017, 10:54 a.m., https://x.com/realDonaldTrump/status/897478270442143744.

the worst idea to have something strong to say, reinforcing our values without pointing any fingers.

I laid out the circumstances for our CEO and his leadership team. At 12:31 p.m., I sent them the following email:

> Every statement the President makes about this council increases the intense scrutiny the media will place on it.
>
> CNBC is currently running a tic-tac-toe-style board with the CEOs who were named and Xs over the ones who have dropped out.
>
> Many in DC media are discussing Larry Summers' piece in the Financial Times this morning, strongly calling out the CEOs still participating in the councils.
>
> A quote from Summers' piece talking about the CEOs choosing to remain on the Council:
>
> **"No advisor committed to the bipartisan American traditions of government can possibly believe he or she is being effective at this point, and all should feel ashamed for complicity in Mr. Trump's words and deeds. I sometimes wonder how they face their children."**
>
> Not suggesting we make any knee-jerk reactions, but our biggest liability here is the President if he continues to keep this story alive (intentionally or unintentionally).
>
> BNA

I still believed there was hope that the phase of this story that focused on the council had nearly passed. The president just needed to stop raising it, and a few more council members needed to issue statements. After all, as pissed off as I was personally, it's not like these CEOs had been the ones brandishing torches in Charlottesville! So, I poured my efforts back into our statement. I wanted to thread the needle between something that would be clear but not newsworthy—the tried-and-true formula: *We're disgusted by the events. Our company has a zero-tolerance policy for bigotry and hate. We are committed to diversity and work within our walls to foster a culture of respect.*

The statement was approved and ready to go. We just had to decide if we wanted to issue it. While waiting to hear back, I turned up the volume on ABC News—one of the five news stations I constantly had running on the TV in my office—to tune into the news coming out of New York.

At 3:20 p.m., President Trump convened an impromptu press conference on infrastructure in the lobby of Trump Tower after a meeting with some of his key economic advisors.

Interesting choice, I thought. It was hard to imagine reporters wanting to discuss infrastructure, given the week we were having as a nation. But sure, I could see the virtue in trying to inject some news to break up the news cycle. Certainly, I kept thinking, his comms team had prepped the press on the focus, and he would be equally prepped to bridge artfully back to his message when questions went off topic.

As expected, the very first question asked by a reporter had nothing to do with infrastructure.

"Mr. President, why do you think these CEOs are leaving your Manufacturing Council?"

Damn. That was a little closer to home than I had anticipated.

At first, the president stayed largely on script. He asserted that CEOs were leaving because he had pressured them in meetings to bring their manufacturing operations back to the US and that some of the more global companies had been looking for an excuse to break off. But as the press conference continued, each question became more pointed, and the president's responses became more combative. He was baited for sure, but increasingly, he was choosing to take the bait.

Then came the fated exchange:

> "Q: Sir. You said there was hatred, there was violence on both sides. Are the—
>
> TRUMP: Well, I do think there's blame. Yes, I think there's blame on both sides. If you look at—If you look at both sides—I think there's blame on both sides. And I have no doubt about it, and you don't have any doubt about it either.
>
> And if you reported it accurately, you would say …
>
> Q: The neo-Nazis started this. They showed up in Charlottesville to protest—
>
> TRUMP: Excuse me, excuse me. They didn't put themselves—you had some very bad people in that group, but you also had people that were very fine people, on both sides."[24]

My jaw dropped. Not because I didn't understand what the president was *trying* to say. But because of what he actually did say. And because I could never, before this moment, imagine a sitting president of the United States saying such a thing.

---

24 "Transcript of Trump's Contentious Aug. 15 Press Conference," ABC News, August 16, 2017, https://abcnews.go.com/Politics/transcript-trumps-contentious-aug-15-press-conference/story?id=49254485.

In a mere seventeen-minute span, I had watched what would become one of the most defining and controversial moments of the next four years of this new president's administration. It was right then that it became clear to me: We were embarking on a new era, and the old systems that American industry was used to operating under were falling by the wayside.

Bzzt-bzzt. Bzzt-bzzt. Bzzt-bzzt. Bzzt-bzzt. As if on cue, my phone began buzzing out of control.

By the time the clock hit 3:40 p.m., I was already fielding incoming from dozens of news outlets. A group called SumofUsAll reached out with a list of more than twenty-eight thousand people who had signed petitions demanding that CEOs step down from advisory councils. Our Washington office was receiving nonstop calls from community members, partners, and even shareholders.

One shareholder who called said, "It is appalling that the CEO of UTC continues to stay on the president's manufacturing council, given the disgusting behavior the president has exhibited with the Charlottesville issue with all the KKK, white nationalists, alt-right, neo-Nazis … This is the complete opposite of UTC and the CEO's message of diversity on the UTC website. I would like to see the CEO walk away from the council right now! If UTC is leading in diversity, then the CEO should feel appalled about the president's behavior!"

In the crush of hostile messages, though, there was also a bright spot. Jen Friedman, then head of issues and crises communications for General Electric (GE), wanted to talk.

GE was UTC's number one competitor. It made jet engines, and so did we. We were at each other's throats in the marketplace, but in this moment, our fortunes were linked. Jen's CEO, Jeff Immelt, was also on the Manufacturing Council, and, much like us, GE was getting buried in incoming calls and messages, especially after the president's latest comments.

So even though we were competitors, it made sense for us to be in lockstep and even broaden our circle. I reached out to Gordon Johndroe, the former senior Bush White House official who was now leading government communications at Boeing, and Matt Perra, who led the same function for Lockheed Martin. We made up a powerhouse brain trust that could see this issue from all sides: Gordon; Jen, a former White House communications alum from the Obama years; Matt, one of the better employee and business communicators in the industry; and me, with my acute understanding of grassroots movements and advocacy from my time with Rev. Jackson. We would share thoughts and updates and pressure-test each other's thinking in real time throughout the next few days. Now that the question of whether to stay on the council or to pull out was reaching a fever pitch, having that group's input and coordination was a godsend.

Meanwhile, internally at UTC, we'd hit a decision point. Some members of Greg's leadership team felt we should stay silent and keep out of the fray. Others felt that even if we wanted to say something, there was no way to adequately respond to the comments made by the president. "He sounded insane," one executive said.

In my mind, our options were clear. Either we would pull out and say why, or we would stay on and say why. A piecemeal statement would no longer meet the moment. I decided to begin drafting a statement for each scenario.

Greg listened to everyone but kept his cards very close to the vest. He was well aware that any leak, even of his preliminary thinking, would be front-page news. He quietly scheduled a meeting of the UTC board of directors for the next day.

Wednesday, August 16, 2017

We received word on the morning of August 16 that Andy Liveris was calling for a council meeting at two thirty that afternoon. I still didn't know where we were heading, and my stomach was in knots. By late that morning, however, Greg announced that he had decided, with the board's blessing, to withdraw from the council. My colleagues and I sprang into action.

Our cross-functional team began reworking the proposed statement I had drafted, carefully choosing each word. The social media team worked on just the right graphic, and the legal team added hedges and poked holes. Finally, it was in Greg's hands to review.

But it wouldn't be that simple.

President Trump had another CEO advisory board in addition to the American Manufacturing Council. The Strategic and Policy Forum was chaired by Steve Schwarzman, CEO of Blackstone. Unbeknownst to the Manufacturing Council members, the Strategic and Policy Forum had called its own meeting for eleven thirty in the morning. During their call, the majority agreed to disband that council because of concerns over President Trump's most recent comments on the Charlottesville events. News of their decision began to leak around 12:50 p.m., just as Schwarzman was sharing the forum's decision with the president.

Tick-tock. The race was on.

At 12:58 p.m., Andy Liveris sent an email to the remaining American Manufacturing Council CEOs marked "URGENT" in all caps. "We need the call asap," it read. "Events are overtaking us with the strategy council decision that just got announced. Please dial in for a 1:15 pm call."

Kevin Kolevar, who headed government affairs for Dow, followed this up with a note to staff at 1:07 p.m., and I flipped it over to Nancy at 1:12 p.m. with the note, "Call is now in 3 mins. Our timeline might have just been moved up ..."

Tick-tock.

Nancy wrote back a minute later, saying, "We're finalizing the statement and will have it out on Twitter in 3 minutes."

But at exactly 1:14 p.m., before the tweet could get off, before the Manufacturing Council could convene, and before I could get the final statement out to a single reporter, President Trump tweeted, "Rather than putting pressure on the businesspeople of the Manufacturing Council & Strategy & Policy Forum, I am ending both. Thank you all!"

In a play to control the narrative, Trump effectively dissolved both councils.

Three minutes later, our statement was published. From there, the next few hours became spin control.

I instructed the media team to go on the offense. We emailed every reporter who had contacted us that week to ensure they'd seen our statement. I followed up with calls to a few influential reporters to let them know on background, PR speak for "as a credible source who they weren't allowed to quote directly," that the CEO of UTC had made the decision hours earlier to resign from the council and had even informed his board.

The coverage was mixed. *POLITICO* noted that Greg's resignation came in a statement that "roughly coincided with Trump's announcement via Twitter that he was disbanding the panel."[25]

---

25 Connor O'Brien, "United Technologies CEO Resigns from Trump Manufacturing Board," *POLITICO Pro*, August 16, 2017, https://subscriber.politicopro.com/article/2017/08/united-technologies-ceo-resigns-from-trump-manufacturing-board-091874.

The *LA Times*, on the other hand, published a piece, saying,

> *Several CEOs issued strong statements condemning racism and bigotry, begging the question of why they hadn't acted earlier. No points for these CEOs.*
>
> *Greg Hayes, United Technologies: Hayes resigned from the jobs panel after Trump announced its dissolution, which leaves unclear what he was resigning from.*
>
> *"The values that are the cornerstone of our culture: tolerance, diversity, empathy and trust, must be reaffirmed by our actions every day," Hayes said, four days after Trump's first statements about Charlottesville placed those values in doubt.*[26]

Dr. George Korn, my former colleague and then communications director for Rev. Jesse Jackson, shot me a text that simply read, "better late than never … :)."

And for all of our tight coordination, GE, UTC, Lockheed, and Boeing all landed in different places. GE issued a statement thirty minutes after ours, in which its CEO, Jeff Immelt, emphasized that he had tendered his resignation earlier in the day. Lockheed went in the complete opposite direction. Matt's CEO, Marillyn Hewson, sent a note to the entire workforce outlining the reasons why she intended to stay the course, noting, "I believe the mission of the advisory council remains critical to our business and the United States, which is why I've decided to remain a member. I feel strongly that the best way to represent our company and our employees is to continue to have a seat at the table."

---

26 Michael Hiltzik, "Column: Courageous or Craven? Ranking the CEOs by How Long It Took Them to Bail on Trump," *Los Angeles Times*, August 17, 2017, https://www.latimes.com/business/hiltzik/la-fi-hiltzik-ceo-rankings-20170817-story.html.

Her note went out three minutes before Trump pulled the plug.

And Boeing. Well, Boeing said nothing.

As I reflected on the previous days' events, I knew one thing for certain: The conventional wisdom that said corporations should keep all things political at arm's length was no longer an option.

I made the following LinkedIn post on my own account, in my own voice, without apology, and without getting prior approval:

> United Technologies decided to resign from the President's advisory council yesterday as a statement that the hatred we've seen and heard these last several days is disgusting and that any even tacit endorsement of it is unacceptable.
>
> As both a Black American and as an employee, I'm proud of my company and our CEO for making that decision in the face of significant business and personal risk. While I prefer our choice, I also respect those who denounced the actions and response, but remained hopeful that they could make a bigger difference by remaining on the council and trying to make change from the inside out.
>
> I don't claim to be a CEO, but I have watched a CEO wrestle with the same type of raw, gripping, hurt and disgust that I have. I have worked for one who has cared about how I'm treated as an employee and who has moved mountains to ensure that I could always feel safe, valued and included inside our company, even if I can't always say the same beyond our walls.
>
> That matters to me.

> Let's not lose sight of the core objective which is to leave this world better than the one we entered—whatever piece of it we can. It's up to all of us to fight for the type of society we want and deserve in the best way that we know how.[27]

My post received more than three hundred likes in the first two days and spurred lots of conversation. I received hate-filled direct messages and emails, and I received encouraging ones. But most importantly, I received messages from people who genuinely appreciated my clarity and personal vulnerability.

Key Learnings:

There were a lot of lessons learned that week. Some were clearly tactical:

- We needed to be faster.
- We needed more coordination and fewer approvals.
- We needed people speaking for us.
- We needed to stay engaged throughout, not just when we had an answer.
- We needed to be proactive.
- We needed thicker skin.

But there was another takeaway from this experience that ran much deeper. For someone who had always strived to "get it right," it was a revelation I hadn't expected. I now knew that while there are a lot of ways to get it right and a lot of ways to get it wrong, what's most important is that you always be your

27 Bradley Akubuiro, "United Technologies Decided to Resign from ... ," LinkedIn, August 17, 2017, https://www.linkedin.com/posts/bradleyakubuiro_united-technologies-decided-to-resign-from-activity-6303961787012251648-4906.

authentic self and allow your humanity to shine through. It's far better to take a values-based stand and let the chips fall where they may than to equivocate and risk being seen as indecisive or, worse, as not walking your walk.

The final lesson of the week came from an unexpected source—the president himself. It was simply this: While you might not be able to control the world around you, you have the power to exert real influence in how you choose to respond to its movements. Understanding that power, I realized, was going to be a game changer for every leader operating in this new era.

While you might not be able to control the world around you, you have the power to exert real influence in how you choose to respond to its movements.

CHAPTER THREE

MY PEOPLE, MY PARTY, AND ME

Americans are at war with themselves. Every difference—whether political, cultural, or personal—is now a battle line, and people are out for blood. But rage isn't the primary emotion driving our divisions. It's actually fear. Fear of displacement, fear of change, fear of what we don't understand. While trying to protect ourselves, our livelihoods, and our way of life, we lash out as a defense mechanism against those who see the world differently than we do, as we believe they intend to do us harm. Understanding this is key to recognizing where the societal land mines are hidden.

We've known for some time that where a person lives, how they earn a living, where they get their information, and where they place their economic priorities will all impact how they view a politician. But today, these also serve as determining factors when it comes to how they perceive your brand's messaging. As stakeholder experts, our job is to recognize the different constituencies out there and make informed decisions on what to say and how to say it, or at the very least know in advance what has the potential to trigger fallout.

This chapter and the one that follows are designed to lift the veil on these disparate constituencies and get to the heart of how the different Americas affect brand perception, a necessary point of reference that will inform the more pragmatic solutions-based content to follow. Being blind to the fact that there are multiple Americas can get you and your company into trouble. And even when you're fully aware of the divisions, it's still easy to play right into an unhelpful narrative if you don't pay close attention to where the specific fault lines are and take care to maintain your integrity while navigating them.

Aba Blankson, chief marketing and communications officer at the National Association for the Advancement of Colored People, has spent years helping organizations thread this needle in some of the most polarized environments imaginable.

"When people and partners are pulling in different directions, the instinct is often to find a middle ground that offends no one," Blankson explains. "In practice, that usually pleases no one. The key to showing up with integrity is not trying to be all things to all people. It is being the same thing to everyone, anchored in a clear set of values and commitments that do not shift with the audience."

This consistency becomes your North Star when stakeholders demand contradictory responses. You can adapt your language and emphasize different elements for different audiences, but your position, your actual stance, remains constant. When you try to be everything to everyone, you end up being nothing to anyone.

PROPORTIONATE PERCEPTION

In 2021, while I was still with Boeing, *The New York Times* reporter David Gelles called me to get my comment on a story he was writing about CEO compensation and how starkly it contrasted with the pay of the average worker. His assertion was that not only had CEO comp gotten out of control but that in many cases, it was not even reflective of the actual performance of the companies these individuals led. To bring this point home, he planned to make an example of Boeing CEO David Calhoun's compensation package totaling $21 million, an amount that he thought seemed excessive given the fact that the company's performance in 2020 had been less than stellar.

In my mind, there was no point in arguing with Gelles. I agreed with his premise that there was, indeed, a massive disparity between the pay of most CEOs and that of the average worker. But I wanted to offer what I believed was an important clarification. I pointed out that the actual value of Dave's package was not, technically speaking, $21 million. I explained that not only had Dave given up the majority of his $1.4 million salary, which was the only guaranteed portion of his compensation, to account for pandemic-related losses but that the vast majority of his compensation was also in the form of restricted stock shares, which were far from guaranteed. The shares were tied to insanely difficult success measures that were not strictly financial, such as getting the MAX airplanes back in service and achieving certification of the new 777X long-range airplane. Of course, the board believed those things were *possible* but hard, and the target compensation was based on the value the company would realize if the CEO they were gambling on could get these things done. If he couldn't, I offered, the vast bulk of his contingent compensation would never come his way. And even if he did meet all the goals set out in his package, it would be years before he received most of his comp, as it wouldn't be released until the multiyear goals were actually accomplished.

The point I was trying to make was that the CEO's compensation was directly proportionate to the value he was bringing to the company, even if it appeared disproportionate to the salaries of

Boeing's rank-and-file workers. Turns out, as true as this point may have been, it was not going to help my case. At all.

Two days later, the front-page story opened with an image of seven CEOs, including Jeff Bezos of Amazon, Disney's Bob Iger, and my guy, Dave Calhoun. The article's lead, its opening kill shot, was directed at us.

"Boeing had a historically bad 2020. Its 737 Max was grounded for most of the year after two deadly crashes, the pandemic decimated its business, and the company announced plans to lay off 30,000 workers and reported a $12 billion loss. Nonetheless, its chief executive, David Calhoun, was rewarded with some $21.1 million in compensation."[28]

Ouch.

But it didn't end there. As I was about to learn, there was a personal price I'd have to pay for my attempt to soften the blow.

On the morning that Gelles's story ran, he co-authored a preview of the piece with fellow *The New York Times* journalist Andrew Ross Sorkin for *DealBook*, the influential daily financial tip sheet Sorkin founded. And in a twist I never would have anticipated, Gelles and Sorkin took the unusual step of blasting a handful of the corporate spokespeople Gelles had contacted while writing the story. I, unfortunately, joined several of my contemporaries in the line of fire.

"Companies battered by the pandemic are handing out enormous pay packages to their C.E.O.s, highlighting the sharp divides in a nation on the precipice of an economic boom, but still wracked by steep income inequality,"[29] the story read.

---

28 David Gelles, "C.E.O. Pay Remains Stratospheric, Even at Companies Battered by Pandemic," *New York Times*, April 24, 2021, https://www.nytimes.com/2021/04/24/business/ceos-pandemic-compensation.html.

29 David Gelles et al., "Why These C.E.O.s Got Paid So Much in the Pandemic," *New York Times*, April 26, 2021, https://www.nytimes.com/2021/04/26/business/dealbook/ceo-pay-pandemic.html.

The section of this teaser piece that addressed my conversation with Gelles started with the header, "It could have been even more," followed by:

> *Boeing wanted to make clear how much money Dave Calhoun "voluntarily elected to forgo to support the company through the Covid-19 pandemic"—some $3.6 million, according to a spokesman. Nonetheless, Calhoun was awarded $21.1 million last year, while Boeing lost $12 billion.*[30]

I had obviously missed the memo. The wealthy would be treated as an organized team of villains, and right or wrong, the perception would forever be that my CEO was a card-carrying member of that supposed cabal.

Not surprisingly, I got lit up both inside the company and out. The experience proved a valuable lesson about the importance of reading the room or, in this case, reading the tenor of the times. People were struggling then, and they continue to struggle now. The divide between the haves and have-nots wasn't going away. As dysfunctional as the system is, it still works quite well for one type of person. And working-class people are tired of seeing the same winners win while they keep feeling the pain of losing.

Knowing your audience is always important, but it's especially critical when you're embroiled in a crisis scenario where time is of the essence. When the hammer is bearing down, you simply don't have the luxury of time to test the waters before jumping into the deep end. Forget focus groups, market surveys, and A/B testing. If you don't already have a solid sense of how your statements are going to be interpreted by certain segments of society, you're asking for trouble.

---

30 Gelles et al., "Why These C.E.O.s Got Paid So Much in the Pandemic."

I'm not saying you should try to be all things to all people. That's literally impossible in our fractured society. But you at least need to know where the fault lines are and understand whether you could be insulting or alienating one audience as you're validating, reassuring, or embracing another.

US VERSUS THEM MEETS CANCEL CULTURE

As a Black American who grew up in an urban environment under trying circumstances, the us-versus-them divide has always been apparent to me. But I didn't really consider how partisan politics had been steadily deepening this divide until I read the book *End of Discussion: How the Left's Outrage Industry Shuts Down Debate, Manipulates Voters, and Makes America Less Free (and Fun),* co-authored by my friend and fellow Northwestern University alum Guy Benson and his colleague Mary Katharine Ham.

When the book first came out in 2015, I was immersed in local DC progressive politics, and I assumed I would gain little from a book by these two conservative journalists and commentators. To be completely honest, I fully expected to find their viewpoints offensive, but I bought the book to support my friend.

The book's premise is that the left has a tendency to police language and behavior and that this was beginning to breed resentment among many Americans. Rather than dismissing the argument, I found myself nodding in agreement as the authors made their case. They argued that shutting down debate by forcing social and professional consequences, which they termed the outrage industry, wasn't just alienating conservatives; it was creating a pressure cooker that couldn't help but explode at some point.

They had my attention, though I'll admit, at the time I thought the warnings were exaggerated. Yes, there were high-profile cases of people losing jobs or public figures taking social media heat over offensive comments; and yes, I had noticed that the list of words one wasn't supposed to use—so-called politically incorrect speech—had been steadily growing over the years, but it didn't feel like there was this burgeoning epidemic of misplaced outrage that the authors were positing. That was until a couple of years later, when I began to feel like Guy and Mary Katherine's book had almost preternaturally predicted the onset of what the right would start calling cancel culture.

Did Progressive Movements Reach Their Tipping Points?

On October 15, 2017, Alyssa Milano famously tweeted #MeToo in response to news reports of sexual abuse allegations against film producer Harvey Weinstein,[31] spurring on what would become the start of a dramatic and, I would like to emphasize, wholly warranted reckoning with widespread misogyny and sexual misconduct throughout American society.

Within hours of that tweet, tens of thousands of women shared their own experiences in solidarity with the #MeToo movement. By the next day, Facebook reported twelve million reactions connected to #MeToo. In 2018 alone, #MeToo was tweeted more than *fifty-five thousand times a day.* The veil had been lifted, and for the first time, women across the socio-economic, regional, racial, professional, and political divides felt empowered to share their experiences with systemic misogyny and sexual abuse in the workplace and beyond.

---

31 Amy Brittain, "Me Too Movement," *Encyclopaedia Britannica*, last modified September 25, 2025, https://www.britannica.com/topic/Me-Too-movement.

Clearly, the #MeToo movement was grounded in the reality that all too many women, and not just a few men, routinely faced inappropriate, if not downright criminal, sexual predatory behavior.

As more and more survivor stories came to light, the hammer came down hard, taking out scores of prominent businesspeople, celebrities, and politicians. CBS CEO Les Moonves and McDonald's CEO Steve Easterbrook were called out for their inappropriate sexual behaviors. And they were not alone. A *TIME* story in June 2018 noted that 414 high-profile executives had been implicated in some type of sexual misconduct over the preceding eighteen months.[32] Celebrities such as comedian Louis C. K. and morning talk show host Matt Lauer were called out for their predatory behavior. And elected officials from both sides of the aisle—including the former Republican governor of Missouri, Eric Greitens, and former US senator from Minnesota, Democrat Al Franken—saw their political careers end abruptly following allegations of sexual impropriety.

Two years after Milano's tweet, bystanders in Minneapolis recorded the brutal murder of George Floyd at the hands of a racist cop, and America entered another intensified cultural moment as conversations about race, equity, and privilege dominated the national discourse.

In retrospect, it's undeniable that as the #MeToo movement picked up steam, its expanding net swept up not just the worst offenders but also some who, in retrospect, were probably more deserving of censure than outright exile. And there's no doubt that the BLM movement, which gained momentum on the heels of the Floyd murder as well as the numerous other incidents of police brutality toward African Americans, engendered justifiable calls for accountability. But in some cases, the targeting went too far, expanding beyond actual bad actors

---

32 Jeff Green, "#MeToo Has Implicated 414 High-Profile Executives and Employees in 18 Months," *TIME*, June 25, 2018, https://time.com/5321130/414-executives-metoo/.

to include those who were perceived as insufficiently enthusiastic allies of the racial justice movement.

We were witnessing the crescendo of the trend Guy and Mary Katharine had warned about years before: a climate in which dissent, hesitation, or even innocent missteps could result in swift and severe consequences—including losing wholesale credibility, stature, and in many cases, careers. Republicans (who are always great at naming things) deemed this phenomenon "cancel culture," and the designation stuck.

The pendulum started to swing in the opposite direction. After years during which the momentum had been on the side of political correctness, the canceling of people with a different point of view no longer felt like a natural extension of inclusion. A growing backlash started to form.

Fast-forward to today, and there's a palatable weariness of anything that can be labeled as politically correct. Movements that once commanded broad support are now struggling to maintain credibility in the face of criticism that they presumably overreached. Across industries and institutions, DEI initiatives are facing not just pushback but outright annihilation. President Trump's January 2025 executive order[33] instructing the dismantling of DEI programs across the federal government was a clear reflection that the pendulum had swung in the opposite direction.

This isn't to say that progressive values are being completely undone. Rather, it's become clear that the intensity of social and linguistic policing triggered an inevitable response from those who felt it was becoming impossible for even well-meaning people to meet

33 "Ending Radical and Wasteful Government DEI Programs and Preferencing," The White House, January 20, 2025, https://www.whitehouse.gov/presidential-actions/2025/01/ending-radical-and-wasteful-government-dei-programs-and-preferencing/.

the standards being set. People who felt they had to walk on eggshells to avoid even an appearance of impropriety are now rejecting those constraints altogether.

In some cases, these rejections of political correctness are manifesting in ways that undermine the very causes that spurred the cultural shifts in the first place. Who can forget the infamous leaked tape of then presidential candidate Donald Trump exclaiming he could grab women "by the pussy" anytime he wants?[34] While many Republicans might have been outraged and even disgusted, that didn't stop Trump from being elected the forty-fifth president of the United States.

Looking back, Guy and Mary Katharine were on to something prescient. They saw the warning signs before many of us did, and while I may have bristled at some of their arguments back then, it's impossible to ignore how their thesis has played out in real time.

The public's weariness of political correctness isn't the only explanation for the polarization of American society. Increasingly, people are feeling that they belong to a demographic that is being left behind.

FEAR OF DISPLACEMENT

It comes as no surprise that, with the proliferation of AI and automation and the constant barrage of media accounts of immigrants pouring into the United States both legally and illegally, people are experiencing feelings of stress, disorientation, and instability that come with a fear of being displaced by technology, outsiders, or both. While some fears are certainly well-founded, others are the result of long-held biases, fears, and purposeful disinformation campaigns.

---

34 Libby Nelson, "'Grab 'Em by the Pussy': How Trump Talked About Women in Private Is Horrifying," *Vox*, October 7, 2016, https://www.vox.com/2016/10/7/13205842/trump-secret-recording-women.

It's important to be able to identify and address legitimate concerns while toning down the unsubstantiated and often dangerous rhetoric, even if these false narratives move the needle in your company's favor.

Future Shock

The term *future shock* was coined by American futurist Alvin Toffler in the 1970 book of the same name that he co-wrote with his wife, Adelaide Farrell. The premise of *Future Shock* was that societies, and the individuals within them, become overwhelmed when technological changes occur too rapidly. Fearing that they can't keep up, people become convinced that technology will be their undoing, rendering their roles and their means of making a living obsolete.

As current times show, these fears are not unfounded.

All you have to do is scroll through LinkedIn or follow the news to see relatable stories about AI and automation taking over jobs. Writers, programmers, graphic artists, and designers are constantly being cautioned that AI fluency—being a proficient so-called prompt engineer—is now a prerequisite if they want to stay current (and employed). Business publications are publishing disconcerting statistics. A *Forbes* piece reported that 60 percent of jobs will require workers to significantly adapt to AI if they want to keep their positions, noting that automation and intelligent systems will become an integral part of every workplace by 2050.[35]

While some professions—such as in healthcare, education, construction, and the skilled trades—are considered more resilient to these disruptive tech changes, Goldman Sachs has predicted that generative AI and robotics will have automated half of all US jobs

---

35 Jack Kelly, "The Jobs That Will Fall First as AI Takes Over the Workplace," *Forbes*, April 25, 2025, https://www.forbes.com/sites/jackkelly/2025/04/25/the-jobs-that-will-fall-first-as-ai-takes-over-the-workplace/.

by 2045.[36] Billionaire hedge fund manager Ray Dalio (a Bully Pulpit International [BPI] client) describes this as part of the changing world order, where technological disruption accelerates the displacement of traditional economic structures faster than new systems can emerge to replace them.[37]

Tech-related displacement fears reach beyond monetary concerns. Some see the potential for gains made toward diversity to fall victim to AI expedience. AI has been called out as providing a convenient (and cost-reducing) avenue for companies to fulfill the lip service they've given to inclusion while bypassing the spirit of actually implementing meaningful changes to prior exclusionary practices.

A great example of this is *Vogue*'s use of an AI-generated model in a 2025 advertisement campaign, which sparked significant controversy in the fashion industry. Rather than hiring diverse talent, critics argued that the magazine artificially generated it. Model and activist Sinead Bovell called this "robot cultural appropriation": the idea that brands can generate diverse identities to tell brand stories without actually employing people from those communities. As Bovell explained, this practice allows companies to create "certain, especially diverse, identities to tell a brand story, even if the person who created the technology isn't of that same identity," effectively depriving real minority models of work opportunities while giving the appearance of inclusion.[38]

---

36 Sophie Kiderlin, "Goldman Sachs Says Generative A.I. Could Impact 300 Million Jobs—Here's Which Ones," CNBC, March 28, 2023, https://www.cnbc.com/2023/03/28/ai-automation-could-impact-300-million-jobs-heres-which-ones.html.

37 Kelly, "The Jobs That Will Fall First."

38 Rebecca Bellan and Dominic-Madori Davis, "The Uproar over Vogue's AI-Generated Ad Isn't Just About Fashion," *TechCrunch*, August 3, 2025, https://techcrunch.com/2025/08/03/the-uproar-over-vogues-ai-generated-ad-isnt-just-about-fashion/.

Immigration Fears

The fear of displacement by immigrants is nothing new. American history is riddled with instances of displacement fears engendering backlashes against immigrants. In the late nineteenth century, as white settlers were seeking opportunities in the American West, fears of economic competition from Chinese immigrants willing to accept lower wages led to the Chinese Exclusion Act of 1882, the first federal law to ban immigration based on race or national origin.[39]

Fear of displacement by immigrants has been a recurring theme in America's history, but the parallels between the present times and what occurred during the Great Depression can't be denied. In the 1930s, many Americans blamed Mexican immigrants for taking away what few jobs and opportunities were available to them, as well as scarce resources. What followed then was a campaign of mass deportations of Mexicans and Mexican Americans, including US citizens.[40]

Nearly a century later, immigrant displacement paranoia seemed to reach an all-time high when, during the September 10, 2024, nationally televised presidential debate, then-candidate Trump repeated the false narrative that Haitian immigrants in Springfield, Ohio, were capturing and consuming family pets: "They're eating the dogs … eating the cats … eating the pets of the people that live there."[41]

The velocity with which this thoroughly debunked racist and xenophobic rumor spread throughout the country brought American

---

39 Erika Lee, *At America's Gates: Chinese Immigration During the Exclusion Era, 1882–1943* (University of North Carolina Press, 2003), 5–10.

40 Francisco E. Balderrama and Raymond Rodríguez, *Decade of Betrayal: Mexican Repatriation in the 1930s* (University of New Mexico Press, 2006), 1–5.

41 Alexandra Ulmer, "At Debate, Trump Shares Falsehoods About Pet-Eating, Infanticide," Reuters, September 11, 2024, https://www.reuters.com/world/us/debate-trump-shares-falsehoods-about-pet-eating-infanticide-2024-09-11/.

discourse about the role of immigrants in American society to an all-time low.

DISTILLING THE FIVE FAULT LINES

As a practical framework, it helps to recognize that none of these fears and divisions are random—they follow predictable fault lines. Five specifically. The **economic divide** pits "haves" against "have-nots," making any action perceived as benefitting the wealthy over the average person vulnerable to populist backlash. The **cultural-political divide** means identity politics and backlash cycles create opposing camps: What delights one side enrages the other. The **tech divide** is perfectly illustrated by views on AI and automation, where some see tools for success while others see instruments of displacement. The **institutional trust divide** reflects eroding faith in media, government, and big business, meaning different audiences will trust (or distrust) your message based on your scale, interests, and perceived power, and more broadly, which institutions they're still willing to believe in. The **information divide** is where people get news from TikTok over *The New York Times*, or choose between MSNBC and FOX. The same communication gets interpreted through completely different information ecosystems, often with vastly different framing. Here's what matters: When you put out messages, reactions from one side of these divides will differ radically from reactions on the other side. Read the room. Know where backlash might originate. And understand that when you step on these fault lines, wittingly or unwittingly, expect the response to be fierce and potentially viral. Cracker Barrel learned this when it attempted brand shifts that felt offensive to conservative populists. These aren't theoretical categories. They're live wires.

FIVE FAULT LINES OF MODERN REPUTATIONAL RISK

TECH DIVIDE
Fears around AI, automation, and potential job loss create significant tension points for brands

CULTURAL-POLITICAL DIVIDE
Identity politics and backlash cycles make neutral positioning increasingly difficult

ECONOMIC DIVIDE
Populist pressure and "haves vs. have-nots" narratives fuel backlash against corporations

INSTITUTIONAL TRUST DIVIDE
Eroding faith in media, government, and big business creates credibility challenges

INFORMATION DIVIDE
Platform collapse & shifting information sources (TikTok > NYT) complicate message control

MANAGING COMMUNICATIONS THROUGH THE DECEPTIONS AND DISCONNECTS

The two Americas, the us-versus-them mentality, and legitimate (and not-so-legitimate) displacement fears divide us in more ways than we can count. How do institutions maintain commitments to fairness and inclusion without alienating a public that is increasingly rejecting perceived overreach? How do communicators craft messages that acknowledge both the necessity of social progress and the very real exhaustion with its byproducts? How can we allay the irrational displacement fears of our audiences while acknowledging that there is a very real transformation happening within the American workforce?

These are the uncharted challenges for anyone involved in leadership or public affairs. And for us communicators, our ability to deliver a message that will be received and not rejected will depend on our understanding of these underlying fears and the visceral responses that certain language or actions can trigger, even inadvertently, for different audiences. To meet this challenge, we must first understand how and where people seek out and receive information.

Key Learnings:

Fear, not rage, drives most divisive reactions. Understanding the underlying anxieties helps you avoid accidentally triggering unnecessary backlash. Reading the room means understanding your audience's economic and cultural context, not just their political preferences.

CHAPTER FOUR

TRUTH VERSUS TRUST

MISINFORMATION IN A HALF-TRUTH, AI-DRIVEN WORLD

We are living in an era where people get to choose their truths. In fact, 70 percent of us get our news from sources that align with our preconceived views.[42] Just think about what this type of information, based on biased perception, means for our jobs as communicators.

Merriam-Webster defines truth as "the body of real things, events, and facts: actuality; the state of being the case: fact."[43] If people *choose* what is true, they are, in essence, ignoring facts in favor of a subjectivity that comports with their chosen reality (oxymoron, anyone?). If someone is going to tell a lie about you or your brand, the thing that will matter most is not whether the allegation has any basis in reality but how much trust your stakeholder audience already has in

42 Gallup and Knight Foundation, *American Views: Trust, Media, and Democracy*, February 15, 2023.

43 *Merriam-Webster*, s.v. "truth," accessed June 19, 2025, https://www.merriam-webster.com/dictionary/truth.

your brand. When it comes to your successful reputation defense, what carries the day won't be objective facts and compelling proofs; it will be how much trust you've either built up in advance or can muster after the fact to shield you from disinformation turning into a full-fledged crisis.

For those seeking to promote a compelling—even if destructive and unfounded—narrative, nothing plays to an audience like a story that plays in their fears while feeding into their political and social agendas. Sensational stories sell. Sensational stories that feed into an existing bias go viral.

THE BOOGEYMAN SELLS PAPERS

On December 13, 2020, the *New York Post* published a story with the provocative headline, "US Companies Riddled with Members of Chinese Communist Party."[44]

As if that headline didn't register high enough on the boogeyman scale, the piece began with this sentence: "As we try to come to terms with the extent of Chinese influence over the Biden family, a leaked database of registered members of the Chinese Communist Party has exposed a mass infiltration of American companies—with serious national security implications."

Although the article was oozing with anti-Biden vitriol, it was difficult to identify as an opinion piece. The *Post* is known for its over-the-top reporting and its even further sensationalized editorials. Although the article belonged to the latter category, this wasn't immediately obvious. Even though there was a small red banner that said "OPINION" just over the headline, the article was written in

---

44 Miranda Devine, "US Companies Riddled with Members of Chinese Communist Party," *New York Post*, December 14, 2020, https://nypost.com/2020/12/13/us-companies-riddled-with-members-of-chinese-communist-party/.

an investigative journalism style. In fact, when, as spokesperson for Boeing—one of the companies singled out in the article—I provided a quote, it was after I was led to believe a reporter was researching a news article.

What followed the provocative headline and unsubstantiated innuendo in the opening salvo were assertions based on old, outdated information designed to lay out a case that the Chinese Communist Party was going to great lengths to embed party loyalists in top US defense and tech companies, part of its long game to reign supreme over the United States and the world. The author, referring to a database of Chinese Communist Party members, was purposefully preying on her audience's fears of a Communist China takeover. She referenced this database as proof of her assertions while admitting that "none of the people listed in the database have been identified as spies ... ," followed by vague references to "mounting concerns in the State Department" and recent "tightened visa rules" for Chinese Communist Party members.

Seemingly by the writer's own admission, there was no *there* there. But still, she played to readers who were predisposed to the notion that the Chinese are out to get us, offering them a lurid twist about how corporations are being dangerously sloppy in preventing this malicious takeover. The writer was simply pandering to a base constituency to reinforce a political agenda, sell a load of papers, and get those revenue-generating digital page views.

UNDERSTANDING WHAT'S GOING TO STICK

You need more than mere assertions to carry the day. For the *New York Post* narrative to stick, the writer needed two things: an interpretation of facts that could support an appearance of impropriety and a public that would buy into the notion that a line had been crossed.

As my friend Raj Shah explains, you have to pay attention to what type of message is going to stick and, just as importantly, what perceptions might be so embedded in our collective psyche that no amount of evidence or spin will change the outcome.

Raj, whose resume includes serving as deputy press secretary for Trump's first term in the White House and later as deputy chief of staff for House Speaker Mike Johnson, ran the Republican National Committee's opposition research division during the 2016 presidential election. His focus was on uncovering anything that could be used against the Democratic candidate, former Secretary of State Hillary Clinton.

In line with this mission, Raj and his colleagues at the Republican National Committee gathered what they considered solid examples of Clinton's alleged mismanagement of the State Department, hoping to start a firestorm of outrage at what they viewed as Secretary Clinton's gross incompetence. But, as Raj tells it, no matter how many compelling anecdotes they gathered, no matter how many Trump surrogates made the rounds with what seemed like solid talking points, the narrative that Clinton was a poor manager just didn't stick. The prevailing view of practically everyone, even those who hated her candidacy, was that Secretary Clinton might be a lot of things, but an ineffective manager wasn't one of them. She and her husband had been in the public light for so long that it would be nearly impossible to change people's perceptions of them. Love her or hate her, Hillary Clinton could not be painted as inept.

But Raj redoubled his efforts and eventually found a way to turn the tide. The opposition research team came up with the idea of exposing the fact that Secretary Clinton had been sending official emails through a private server located in the basement of her home, something that could be spun as irresponsible at best and endangering the security of the country at worst. The story stuck, and its legs have proven to be long. While polling showed that people don't associate the Clintons with incompetence, many do associate them with scandal, self-dealing, and at times, loose judgment. So, right or wrong, it was easy to see the server incident as more of the same. It played right into her greatest vulnerability.

From Raj's perspective, the mission was accomplished. He had his smoking gun, and the backlash it created took on a life of its own.

STARBUCKS CONFRONTS SOCIAL MEDIA DISINFORMATION

Once the public gloms on to a belief, it's incredibly hard to change the perceptions. And since social media gives everyone a platform to influence public opinion, it's easier than ever for disinformation to be posted, shared, and turn viral at lightning speed. Factor in the reality that posts can remain online and searchable in perpetuity, and it's nearly impossible to break through all the noise to set the record straight. If your company gets caught up in a negative social media firestorm, you'll have to pick your battles and ride out the storm.

This is something the Starbucks leadership understands all too well.

Starbucks, the world's largest coffeehouse chain with more than forty thousand stores across the globe, found itself embroiled in a controversy that escalated into a damaging boycott,[45] all because of the rapid proliferation of half-truths and outright lies on social media.

45 Natalie Sherman, "Starbucks Blames 'Misrepresentation' After Israel Gaza Protests," BBC News, December 20, 2023, https://www.bbc.com/news/business-67777506.

On October 9, 2023, two days after the October 7 Hamas invasion of Israel and massacre of 1,200 men, women, and children, Starbucks Workers United, the union working to organize Starbucks baristas in the US, posted "Solidarity with Palestine!" on X, formerly known as Twitter. The post included the union's logo, which to the untrained eye looked deceptively similar to the Starbucks logo, making the post appear to many like an official company statement. Even though the union took the post down within forty minutes and union organizers claimed that it was made by a rogue employee without the organization's knowledge or consent, it was too late. The bell had been rung. The pro-Palestine post spread rapidly across the internet, creating a domino effect that would end up in a worldwide Starbucks boycott that would damage the company's brand and its financial health.

Starbucks, seeking to distance itself from the post, issued a blanket statement condemning all violence in the region. The company also filed a lawsuit against the union, claiming trademark infringement for using its logo without permission.

Then, someone posted a photo of a uniformed Israel Defense Forces (IDF) soldier holding a rifle in one hand and a cup of Starbucks coffee with the familiar green and white mermaid logo in the other. But there was just one problem … the image wasn't real. The photo had been altered to add a Starbucks cup to the image, and it was disseminated to bolster the baseless rumor that Starbucks was providing funds to the IDF. And it worked. The rumor was accepted as fact, and the photo was widely shared. This was the case despite the fact that Starbucks has never given a dime to the IDF or, for that matter, any government fighting force.

Pro-Palestinian activists and organizations had been looking to make examples of US companies that supported Israel and took this opportunity to ride the wave of the Starbucks controversy, an ironic choice given the fact that Starbucks has close to two thousand locations throughout the Middle East but hasn't had a single store in Israel since 2003.

COUNTERING LIES, RUMORS, AND VITRIOL

Mis- and disinformation are both as old as time, but what is new is their speed and the range they travel. The key is to know your audience and what they care about in relation to you. What's most visible isn't always what is most dangerous. What's more important than what is said is what people believe. If false information is spread about you that runs counter to what your stakeholders want to believe about you or the story you tell about yourself, you have an issue. There are lots of ways to counter false narratives, but the right answer is rarely hand-to-hand combat. The only true defense is for people to love you so much that they choose not to believe the untrue things that they hear. Why? Because it's not actually about truth, it's about trust.

The only true defense is for people to love you so much that they choose not to believe the untrue things that they hear. Why? Because it's not actually about truth, it's about trust.

It's important to be strategic about how and where to combat the lies, rumors, and baseless vitriol. Since you'll never be able to play Whac-A-Mole with every single image or post, you need to find a way to reject damaging falsehoods and broadly assert what's true. To do that, you have to step back and figure out where your greatest vulnerabilities are and what people need to understand from you if you want to keep their trust. You need to understand what made it so easy for people to buy into the lies about your brand and what was driving such a high degree of distrust.

With Starbucks, you could look at how the brand had, in many ways, drifted away from its original roots. The company created great brand affinity early on by establishing a unique experience that felt authentic. It encouraged community. You'd go to a Starbucks, grab a hot (or cold) cup o' Joe, and chill with your friends. The Starbucks brand was about connecting, relating, and vibing with like-minded people.

But over time, that image had given way to one of long lines at the drive-through with stressed-out soccer moms waiting impatiently to order their double skinny chai lattes as the suit in the sports car ahead was picking up her double espresso. Add the fact that Starbucks wasn't exactly thrilled about its baristas forming a union, and the door was open for negative perceptions about the brand to take off.

But the unfortunate truth was that the biggest driver for the lies and the primary reason the boycott took off with such ferocity and velocity was anti-Semitism. Howard Schultz, the former CEO of Starbucks, is a very prominent and successful Jewish business leader who has always been public about his heritage and his support for Israel. The mere fact that Schultz was affiliated with Starbucks was enough to bolster the belief that the conspiracy theories and lies about the brand must be true.

Starbucks began putting its current leadership team on offense, increasing its visibility in both traditional and more modern forms of media. And under new leadership, the company has begun refocusing on its core mission. As CEO Brian Niccol explained about this phase, "We need to get what I would call the soul of the business back and this connection back. We are having to reintroduce the brand to people." He emphasized, "People love Starbucks, but I've heard from some customers that we've drifted from our core, that we've made it harder to be a customer than it should be." His push to reinstate elements of the company's roots, labeled "Back to Starbucks," aligns with the sense of community and connection that made people fall in love with the brand in the first place. And that strategy is producing a lot of success for the company.

AI AS DISINFORMATION ACCELERATOR

This chapter opened with the premise that people get to choose their truths. But what happens if truth becomes unprovable, and lies appear incontrovertible? This is precisely what's happening with the increased use of AI in disinformation campaigns.

AI can help amplify false narratives in unprecedented and potentially dangerous ways. This is a point driven home by cybersecurity company Alethea's CEO, Lisa Kaplan. Lisa shared with me an Alethea report titled *What to Do When a State Actor Targets You*, which presents a harrowing tale of the use of AI in a coordinated state-sponsored disinformation campaign.

The Fighter Jet Takedown That Never Happened

In June 2025, Israeli airstrikes hit Iran. In response, Russian, Iranian, and Chinese actors spread false claims that multiple F-35s had been shot down and a pilot captured in Iran. The carefully coordinated disinformation was spread using a combination of AI-generated images, old crash photos, recycled videos from video games, and entirely fabricated news reports, all designed to seed doubt in US military superiority and fracture global defense alliances.

The related content had more than one hundred thousand views within hours, and some of it was pushed further by influencers with government ties, creating widespread confusion. The result was major pressure on the US government and defense firms to respond to something that never actually happened.

This kind of content would have taken weeks or months to fabricate five years ago. Today, it can be made and amplified in minutes, at zero cost and with global reach.

As Lisa pointed out, disinformation campaigns follow a playbook. First, a false claim shows up in fringe media. Then, it's echoed by pseudo-journalists, picked up by bots, translated into think tank language, and ultimately laundered into mainstream visibility. By the time your comms team spots it on X, it's been optimized for search engines, inserted into AI training data, and cited in multiple semi-legit articles. The actors perpetuating the F-35 hoax followed this playbook to a *T*.

This isn't chaos. It's choreography. And the only way to combat it is by having already laid a foundation of trust.

TRUST IS THE REAL MOAT

Disinformation has nothing to do with truth and almost everything to do with trust. When stakeholders see a rumor—whether on X, Telegram, or TikTok—they won't wait for *Snopes* or CNN to debunk it. They'll think about your company's track record. Have you been clear about your values? Have you built credibility in their channels? Have you made the right friends in advance? Have you engaged in constant and consistent values communication? That's how you build a moat.

Lisa said it best: "The first time to have that conversation is not the day you get targeted. You have to live your values year-round."

Key Learnings:

Truth and trust are different currencies. In a crisis, facts are important, but trust is king.

The only defense against disinformation is building such strong stakeholder relationships that people give you the benefit of the doubt when they hear negative things about you.

AI has turned disinformation into a precision weapon, but it's also given communicators unprecedented tools to fight back.

CHAPTER FIVE

BATTLE LINES DRAWN

AVOIDING CASUALTY IN THE CULTURE WARS

It may look like I've been painting a pretty bleak picture of corporate comms in the current age of issues. I've talked about how a divided America is fueling the culture wars and how the so-called anti-woke movement is creating an environment in which companies, and the people who run them, are running scared or clamming up. Add the proliferation of misinformation, and it would be easy to think the best course of action is to lie low and bury your head in the sand.

But I'm here to advocate for going in the opposite direction. As I always tell the leaders that I counsel: *You have to figure out where you stand and then actually stand there.*

If you do this thoughtfully, consistently, and with a clear purpose in mind, not only will you avoid becoming a culture war casualty; you'll also find that you've garnered the respect of your stakeholders and even many of your detractors.

Earlier, I pointed to the rapid dismantling of the DEI movement as one of the most significant markers of the transition from the age of impact to the age of issues. But the lessons of DEI's rise and fall can also set the groundwork for its resurrection, albeit in a version that is more thoughtfully aligned with what those advocating for inclusion truly aim to accomplish.

D-E-I DOESN'T HAVE TO D-I-E

It was January 10, 2024, a few days after the cabin door on an Alaska Airlines Boeing 737 MAX 9 malfunctioned following the plane's takeoff from Portland. Elon Musk had just ripped on Boeing in two tweets with the baseless claims that the incident happened, somehow, because of Boeing's commitment to DEI.

First tweet: Do you want to fly in an airplane where they prioritized DEI hiring over your safety? That is actually happening.[46]

Second tweet: People will die due to DEI.[47]

The tweets were accompanied by references to Boeing policies and statements linking DEI metrics to executive compensation.

I was livid.

I had worked at that company. I had stayed close to the team I'd watched live and breathe safety every single day. I knew the leadership; I knew the engineers; I knew how hard they'd fought to rebuild trust. I was proud of how far Boeing had come. And here was Elon Musk, whose company SpaceX was a direct competitor of Boeing, carelessly

46 Elon Musk (@elonmusk), "Do you want to fly in an airplane where they prioritized DEI hiring over your safety? That is actually happening," X (formerly Twitter), January 10, 2024, https://x.com/elonmusk/status/1745158868676546609.

47 Elon Musk (@elonmusk), "People will die due to DEI," X (formerly Twitter), January 10, 2024, https://x.com/elonmusk/status/1745159785144594547.

blaming a safety incident on diversity. Without evidence, without accountability, and without a single ounce of shame.

But this wasn't just about Musk's self-serving crusade against a competitor or even against the egalitarianism of DEI. It was about the wave of cosigns his words had ignited. Seemingly overnight, every aviation or transportation failure was being blamed on DEI, as if diversity was the root of all our fears and problems. As if talented, capable professionals had no business being in the room if they didn't fit a specific profile.

This "blame diversity" narrative spread across social media, eventually making its way into the mainstream with the sloganized resentment: "D-E-I must D-I-E." That sentiment was soon echoed by a cast of powerful figures. Conservative activist Edward Blum, fresh off his Supreme Court victory ending affirmative action in college admissions, turned his sights on eliminating the push for diversity in corporate America. Billionaire Bill Ackman used his platform to push anti-DEI narratives across business and academia. Stephen Miller, Trump advisor turned head of the conservative America First Legal Foundation, began building the legal infrastructure to sue companies over race-conscious policies. Influencer Robby Starbuck turned social media into a conservative outrage machine. And then came President Donald Trump 2.0.

As soon as he returned to office, President Trump began to lean in hard. He issued executive orders targeting DEI in federal agencies, cut funding from schools and universities allegedly promoting what he calls Marxist race theory, and pulled research grants from programs that prioritize diversity in hiring or in perspective. He even blamed the January 2025 deadly midair collision between an army helicopter and an American Airlines commuter flight over the Potomac River on DEI.

No evidence. No nuance. Just blame. (To its credit, American Airlines itself handled the entire episode with grace, humility, and efficacy.)

All of this misinformation and disinformation seems to come from one place: fear. The rapid proliferation of DEI initiatives in the early 2020s resulted in a segment of the population that was used to feeling included—if not in control—suddenly feeling desperately left behind. It's easy to see how DEI could become the scapegoat for everything: layoffs, missed promotions, corporate failures, and even in-flight tragedy.

In retrospect, this backlash may have been inevitable. The early waves of post-2020 DEI programs weren't always implemented with care. In the rush to show progress, some companies built systems that excluded rather than included, that signaled who belonged without truly bringing everyone along.

Parents who hadn't given diversity a second thought were now worried that their kids wouldn't get a fair shot at an education, at a job, or at a promotion because of something entirely outside of their control, such as the color of their skin or their gender. That's enough to get anyone riled up. I get it. But here's the thing: DEI was never meant to replace anyone. DEI was never about narrowing the funnel. On the contrary, it was meant to *expand* the number of seats at the table.

But in the process of realizing this ambition, companies were woefully unclear about what DEI meant to them in the context of their values and the constructs of their unique cultures. In a course correction gone awry, some companies are now making the opposite mistake, abandoning diversity initiatives entirely in their haste to distance themselves from controversy or even out of fear of legal repercussions. What's needed isn't abandonment but evolution in how companies frame and implement the decidedly American principle of equity within their organizations. This evolution begins with precision in language. Companies need to articulate exactly what they mean by "diversity" and "inclusion." Forget the generic mission statements and empty buzzwords. Companies must determine what they truly stand for, and if that includes diversity and inclusion, they need to define what those words mean to them using language that reflects their actual values and culture.

If DEI is going to die, let it be the abbreviation and not the action. Call it talent and inclusion. Call it belonging. Call it opportunity. I don't care what you call it, just make sure it's *real.* Make sure it's *thoughtful.* And make sure it's something people can understand and believe in.

True inclusion doesn't push anyone out; it opens doors wider to allow more people to walk through. If this is what you believe, then say so. And if this is what you're saying, then act accordingly.

As my former boss Rev. Jackson would always say, "The underdog can win when the playing field is even, the rules are public, the goals are clear, the referees are fair, and the score is transparent. Fair rules make America great."

A CALL FOR CONSISTENCY IN CONVICTIONS

There is power in drawing a line in the sand, in knowing who your company is and what values it holds at its core.

The alternative to standing up for your core values is wavering, like I did during Charlottesville, intellectualizing the issues by weighing the pros and cons of advising your company leaders to declare who they are and what they believe. If your convictions tell you that white supremacists should not be rallying around a Confederate statue while chanting racist and anti-Semitic slogans and that your company executives should not pick that moment to stand next to people who are emboldening them, then say so. Your brand will be stronger for it, and your stakeholders will feel reassured by your clarity.

Where Vision Meets Risk: Mapping Your Moves

HIGH PUBLIC VISIBILITY

LOW VALUE ALIGNMENT | HIGH VALUE ALIGNMENT

HIGH VISIBILITY, LOW ALIGNMENT	HIGH VISIBILITY, HIGH ALIGNMENT
One-off political or activist partnerships Support for controversial ballot initiatives ***Flashpoint Zone: Requres Strategic Air Cover***	STEM initiatives in HQ city Sustainability investments rooted in your supply chain ***Sweet Spot: Lean in with Confidence***
LOW VISIBILITY, LOW ALIGNMENT	**LOW VISIBILITY, HIGH ALIGNMENT**
Performative marketing tie-ins Unfocused charitable donations ***Dead Zone: LIttle Upside, Vulnerable to Critique***	Nonprofit capacity building for historically excluded groups Workforce pipeline programs ***Low-Risk, High-Impact: Great for Building Long-Term Trust***

LOW PUBLIC VISIBILITY

DYLAN MULVANEY AND THE CRISIS THAT NEVER WAS

It's April 2023. A globally recognized brand partners with transgender influencer, Dylan Mulvaney. The backlash is swift and merciless. Social media explodes. Conservative voices call for boycotts. High-profile figures slam the company for "going woke." Stock prices wobble.

You probably think you know exactly what company I'm talking about, a beverage company that dominated crisis management case studies for months.

But I'm not talking about that company at all. I'm talking about Nike.

Here's what most people missed: Nike also partnered with Dylan Mulvaney for a major brand campaign. Same influencer. Same timing. Nearly identical backlash.

Olympic swimmer Sharron Davies called Nike's move "a kick in the teeth." Caitlyn Jenner slammed the company for "going woke."[48] Conservative social media erupted with boycott threats and Nike gear being torched. Sound familiar? Absolutely.

But what was unique about Nike's approach was that it never flinched.

Instead of scrambling into damage control mode or distancing itself from its own campaign, Nike doubled down. No apologies. No backtracking. Nike didn't just keep the campaign running; it posted a pinned comment on Instagram instructing customers to "Be kind, be inclusive"[49] and made it perfectly clear: *This is who we are, and we're not changing course because you're upset.*

The results speak for themselves. Nike's stock dipped a few points initially, but its sales remained resilient in the months that followed. More importantly, it maintained credibility with its core customer base and avoided the perception of being a company with no backbone.

This wasn't Nike's first rodeo. In 2018, Nike made Colin Kaepernick the face of its thirtieth anniversary "Just Do It" campaign. Nike

---

48 Chantz Martin, "Nike Responds to Backlash Over Dylan Mulvaney Partnership, Instructs Customers to 'Be Kind, Be Inclusive,'" April 7, 2023, https://www.foxnews.com/sports/nike-responds-to-backlash-over-dylan-mulvaney-partnership-instructs-customers-to-be-kind-be-inclusive.

49 Martin, "Nike Responds to Backlash."

knew that hiring Kaepernick, whose kneeling during the national anthem to protest systemic racism and police brutality had cost him his NFL career, would be controversial. And it wasn't wrong. Protesters burned Nike shoes in their driveways. President Trump weighed in with criticism. Conservative politicians called for boycotts. Nike's stock took a hit.

People can accept disagreeing with you, but what they will never accept is hypocrisy.

But Nike stood firm, and the payoff was both swift and significant: a 31 percent spike in online sales within five days of the campaign launch. But the deeper win was about brand integrity. Nike showed in 2018 that it would rather lose customers who didn't share its values than abandon those values for short-term comfort. And it showed that same consistency in conviction again in 2023 with the Mulvaney campaign.

The lesson is clear. Conviction pays. Waffling costs everything. Nike easily could have retreated, but it ultimately would have lost customers on both sides. Instead, Nike kept its core base and even earned respect from people who disagreed but admired the company's consistency.

People can accept disagreeing with you, but what they will never accept is hypocrisy.

CRACKER BARREL'S FAILED ATTEMPTS AT QUIET APPEASEMENT

Sometimes, hypocrisy rears its head in the form of appeasement. Like many companies in the early 2020s, Cracker Barrel took a public stance about its commitment to diversity and inclusion in the workplace. The chain transparently touted its DEI commitments on its website and in corporate communications, signaling a shift toward broader inclusivity.

As the political climate changed, Cracker Barrel quietly scrubbed its website and other owned media of overt references to diversity and inclusion initiatives. Even though the move was meant to go unnoticed, it didn't take long for media and advocacy groups to uncover the changes and vilify the company for abandoning its commitments without explanation.[50]

But Cracker Barrel's appeasement strategy didn't end there. In August 2025, the company attempted another quiet transformation, this time dropping its iconic "old-timer" figure and barrel from its logo as part of a broader modernization effort. The backlash was swift and severe. Right-wing figures online stoked outrage, the stock plummeted 12 percent, and customer visits fell 8 percent.[51] Within days, even President Trump weighed in, congratulating the company when it reverted to the old logo: "All of your fans very much appreciate it."

The company ended up alienating its allies while failing to appease its critics. First, it lost credibility with diversity advocates by quietly abandoning DEI commitments. Then, it lost its traditional customer base by trying to modernize its brand identity. Adding insult to injury, both the diversity rollback and the logo change became major stories, which was exactly what Cracker Barrel wanted to avoid. The company ultimately suspended its entire $700 million transformation plan, demonstrating the costs of trying to be everything to everyone while standing for nothing.

---

50 Samantha Delouya and Ramishah Maruf, "Cracker Barrel Quietly Removes DEI and Pride Pages from Its Website After Logo Upheaval," CNN, August 29, 2025, https://www.cnn.com/2025/08/28/business/cracker-barrel-removed-dei-and-pride-website.

51 Ramishah Maruf, "Cracker Barrel Changed Its Logo. Then Visits Tumbled," CNN, September 18, 2025, https://www.cnn.com/2025/09/17/business/cracker-barrel-stock-earnings.

CONSISTENCY AND STRENGTH: STANDING UP FOR STAFF

Like the country as a whole, US companies were shaken by the tectonic shift brought on by the Supreme Court's 2022 decision in *Dobbs v. Jackson Women's Health Organization*[52] overturning *Roe v. Wade*.[53] The *Dobbs* ruling, which erased fifty years of advocacy on the issue of women's body autonomy, was more than a legal shift for those of us counseling companies with facilities around the country. It was a five-alarm fire.

The repercussions of the decision were daunting for employers with a workforce spanning several states. Their employees would no longer have uniform protections. Instead, each state would decide whether and to what extent a woman could exercise her right to reproductive self-determination. If a company had previously offered abortion access as part of its benefits package, the *Dobbs* ruling meant that some hard decisions had to be made. Do you cancel those services in states where it's now banned? Do you fund cross-state travel for employees seeking care? What happens if you're sued for doing so? Can you cover these services for some employees but not others? And if you go that route, can you still claim to have a consistent values framework?

It was complicated. It was high stakes. It was a leadership moment.

Some companies met the moment. They said, "This is who we are. This is what we stand for." They didn't just speak to their values; they backed them up with benefits, with policy, and with action.

Others chose to stay quiet. And often, it wasn't the companies you'd expect.

---

52 *Dobbs v. Jackson Women's Health Organization*, 597 U.S. 215 (2022).

53 *Roe v. Wade*, 410 U.S. 113 (1973).

I worked with one organization that had made support for women's health, particularly maternal health, a central part of its brand, loudly celebrating this support as a differentiator in the marketplace. But when *Dobbs* hit and the pressure mounted, it equivocated. It decided to let leaders across its markets determine how to handle the issue and quietly scaled back access to abortion services.

To be clear, I'm not here to tell any company what position to take on abortion. But the disconnect between what these particular employees believed they were promised and how their employer responded in this pivotal moment was glaring. It exposed the real question underneath all the rhetoric: Do your values actually mean something when they're put to the test?

This was a national crisis, and for many organizations, it was a reputational one, too. In crisis situations, you can bet that people are going to pay close attention. Not just to what you say but to how you say it and how loudly.

Several companies chose to update their policies, but they did it quietly. No *Wall Street Journal* op-ed. No big public statement. Just a direct memo to the impacted employees in specific geographies. No broader announcement, no culture war invitation, no press cycle.

And in many cases, it worked.

They honored their commitment to their employees while avoiding unnecessary backlash. They made good on their values but did so with precision and intent, not performative declarations.

Some companies even changed their policies without saying a word about it. The only way to find out what your benefits covered was to reach out to HR and ask directly. And again, I'm not saying that was the right or wrong move. I'm saying every company had to figure it out—quickly.

PROACTIVE OR REACTIVE: TAKE CARE OF YOUR EMPLOYEES

Dobbs didn't come out of nowhere. Legal scholars had flagged it as a likely flash point for years. Companies had roughly two years to prepare. Some used the time, while others got caught flat-footed. And those that were unprepared found themselves scrambling to reconcile risk, compliance, values, and expectations under a national spotlight. There is no doubt that the companies that played an offensive game, that anticipated the possibility of an overturn of *Roe* and developed a playbook for addressing the fallout in accordance with their core values, weathered this storm better than those that didn't.

There are going to be times when you don't have forewarning, when circumstances demand swift and immediate action following an unanticipated event. In those instances, living your values requires showing up for your employees simply because they need you to and because it's the right thing to do.

Over a May weekend in 2022, a white man carrying an automatic rifle with the N-word painted across the barrel made his way to a grocery store in a predominantly Black neighborhood of Buffalo and opened fire. Of the thirteen people shot, eleven were Black.

If you treated the following Monday morning in the workplace like any other, you missed the mark. Because for almost every Black person, it felt like anything but business as usual. As I explained in my *Inc.* article shortly following the incident:

For your Black colleagues, the logic goes like this: If a man is willing to pick up a gun and kill 10 complete strangers out of race-fueled hatred, is it really that much of a stretch to assume that there are people in our own workplaces, some of whom we see every day, who also harbor a similar type of resentment? Maybe they would never point a gun at me, but would they leave me off of a meeting invite? Pass me up for a promotion? Talk badly about me to others? Skip my strengths and focus my review around my weaknesses?[54]

As an employer, a leader, and someone intent on putting your actions where your values lie, it's important to go beyond the usual "thoughts and prayers" party line. Avoid issuing just another blanket statement that condemns all acts of hatred or that reinforces your "zero tolerance for hatred." Your employees don't need your platitudes. They need your support and your compassion. If you're going to make a public statement, make it count. Call out white supremacy by name and state unequivocally that it is wrong. And then, show your concern for your employees' safety and success in the quieter, more private places where they live and work. Offer time off and free counseling. Create a safe space where employees can raise concerns about race issues in the workplace without fear of repercussion. And whatever you do, don't expect praise for doing the right thing. This is what it means to be a strong leader. This is the part of your value proposition that requires walking your talk.

THE CASE FOR CORPORATE ACTIVISM

The culture wars yield real battles with real consequences for real people. But they're not the only threat to your company's future. Sometimes, the most existential fight isn't about society; it's about your license to operate as you choose. There are times when you have no choice but to go to the mattresses in order to preserve your company, its people, and its culture.

---

54 Bradley Akubuiro, "Black People Were Targeted and Massacred in Buffalo Last Weekend. This Week Isn't Business as Usual," *Inc.*, May 17, 2022, https://www.inc.com/bradley-akubuiro/black-people-were-targeted-massacred-in-buffalo-this-weekend-this-week-isnt-business-as-usual.html.

"Be the Activist in Your Own Stock"

In 2018, two heavyweight activist investors, Daniel Loeb of Third Point and Bill Ackman of Pershing Square, took sizable stakes in UTC. Their goal: Pressure CEO Greg Hayes to break up the company.

At the time, UTC was a sprawling industrial conglomerate. The activists believed the company's value was being obscured by its overly complex multi-industrial structure and claimed that breaking it into three standalone businesses could unlock as much as $20 billion in shareholder value.[55] The proposed split: Carrier (climate controls and security), Otis (elevators and escalators), and the aerospace business (Pratt & Whitney combined with Rockwell Collins).

Loeb's firm alone had a $1 billion stake and made its intentions clear in a public letter: "We invested in United Technologies not for what it is today but for what it could become."[56]

Inside the company, it triggered a very different conversation. There were real concerns about what would be lost—most notably, the internal career mobility that had made UTC such a compelling place to grow. You could work in space, aerospace, building technology, and climate solutions, all without ever leaving the company. That connectedness mattered to a lot of people.

But activist investors aren't in it for mobility or legacy. They're in it for the returns.

---

55 Benjamin C. Esty and Daniel Fisher, "United Technologies Corp.: Are the Parts Worth More Than the Whole?," Harvard Business School Spreadsheet Supplement 220-714, November 2019.

56 Svea Herbst-Bayliss, "Hedge Fund Chief Daniel Loeb Opposes United Technologies-Raytheon Merger," Reuters, June 28, 2019, https://www.reuters.com/article/business/hedge-fund-chief-daniel-loeb-opposes-united-technologies-raytheon-merger-idUSKCN1TT1XC/.

As with any company facing activist pressure, we had to walk a tightrope. There were moments of alignment. There were moments of tension. But Greg Hayes was unwavering in his position.

He said it over and over again: "The way you beat an activist is by helping Wall Street understand that *you* are the activist in your own stock."

He meant it. And he backed it up.

Yes, UTC ultimately did split into three businesses. But then came the twist that no one, especially not Loeb or Ackman, had anticipated: Greg engineered a merger of the newly independent aerospace business with Raytheon, forming what would become Raytheon Technologies (now RTX), one of the largest aerospace and defense companies in the world.

Loeb blasted the deal publicly, saying the merger made neither strategic nor financial sense. He called it a victory for "empire building" and accused Hayes of "illogical" behavior.[57]

But here's the thing: It wasn't irrational at all.

Greg had the master plan in his head the whole time. And in that moment, he wasn't reacting to activists; he was outmaneuvering them.

He became the architect of a Fortune 50 powerhouse. And he did it boldly, with clarity of purpose, and through masterful engagement and coordination. Greg stuck to a principle that still rings in my head today: Be the activist in your own stock, or someone else will do it for you.

---

57 "Third Point's Loeb Slams United Technologies-Raytheon Deal," *Gulf Times*, accessed October 17, 2025, https://www.gulf-times.com/story/635340/third-points-loeb-slams-united-technologies-raytheon-deal.

Key Learnings:

People can accept mistakes and even stances they disagree with, but they can't accept hypocrisy. "Figure out where you stand and stand there."

Always be the activist within your organization, or someone else will.

G. K. Chesterton wrote in 1911, as Europe was gripped by rising militarism and hatred, that "the true soldier fights not because he hates what is in front of him, but because he loves what is behind him." He understood something that today's corporate leaders must embrace: The most powerful activism isn't driven by animosity toward your critics or competitors but by fierce devotion to your company, your people, and your mission. When you fight from love rather than hate—when your purpose is clear and your resolve unwavering—you don't just survive the battle; you transcend it.

The most powerful activism isn't driven by animosity toward your critics or competitors but by fierce devotion to your company, your people, and your mission.

CHAPTER SIX

BREAKING NEWS, BREAKING TRUST

SURVIVING THE MODERN MEDIA GAUNTLET

There was a time in the not-too-distant past when traditional media was widely considered the fourth estate, a reference to its role in ensuring transparency in government and as a check on abuses of power. These were the days when the nation tuned into broadcast icons such as Edward R. Murrow and Walter Cronkite (considered to be "the most trusted man in America") for their news.

The public counted on newspapers like *The New York Times* (considered *the* newspaper of record for its meticulous story indexing) and *The Wall Street Journal*, as well as independently run local papers, to provide reliable reporting on the events of the day. Opinion pieces—anything that went beyond answering the who, what, when, where, and why of journalism—were clearly marked as such, making them easily distinguishable from news reporting. Print and broadcast media may have had liberal or conservative bents, but these political orientations largely manifested themselves in clearly designated editorial pages.

Today, traditional media has lost much of its magnetism. Families no longer gather at the TV promptly at six to watch the evening news or sit around the breakfast table poring over the daily paper. The digital age has opened the door for new entrants into the once-insulated world of news gathering and dissemination. New media—including Substacks, social media influencers, video-sharing platforms, podcasts, and streaming services—have provided increasingly sophisticated ways for user-generated content to draw attention away from more traditional news organizations. Influencer reach far surpasses mainstream news consumers in terms of volume. Citizen journalists can live stream news as it happens straight from their smartphones and gain credibility and even notoriety in the process. Darnella Frazier, the teenager who filmed George Floyd's murder on her smartphone, was awarded an honorary Pulitzer Prize for her citizen journalism.[58]

By the early 2020s, 88 percent of Americans were getting their news through digital devices, while only a third said they often turn to TV for information and a paltry 26 percent said they get any news at all from print sources.[59]

There is still enormous value in engaging with print and broadcast reporters when it comes to heightening your influence across multiple media channels. But the key now is in understanding how to leverage the credibility of traditional media as a validator in conjunction with the reach and direct-to-audience access of new media.

---

58 Joe Hernandez, "Darnella Frazier, Who Filmed George Floyd's Murder, Wins an Honorary Pulitzer," NPR, June 11, 2021, https://www.npr.org/2021/06/11/1005601724/darnella-frazier-teen-who-filmed-george-floyds-murder-wins-pulitzer-prize-citati.

59 "News Platform Fact Sheet," Pew Research Center Journalism & Media, September 25, 2025, https://www.pewresearch.org/journalism/fact-sheet/news-platform-fact-sheet/.

VALIDATION OVER REACH: THE RE-EXPANDING ROLE OF TRADITIONAL MEDIA

There continues to be tremendous value in cultivating and maintaining relationships with traditional media outlets. The opinion elites at the top of the talking-head food chain, who often lead the conversations regarding finance and public policy, regularly consult *The New York Times*, *The Wall Street Journal*, *Bloomberg*, and *Reuters* to glean market insights as they pore over data to fuel their points of view. It's a continuous loop of stories that fuels responses, encouraging follow-ups and subsequent inquiries that, in turn, fuel more responses, all while serving to bolster reader and viewer metrics. Influence the narrative here when trying to address traditional powerbrokers.

New media take their cues from these tried-and-true sources. Influencers rehash and repurpose mainstream reporting, often featuring *The New York Times* article or broadcast news story on a split screen to bolster the credibility of their own viewpoints.

But probably the most forward-looking reason to work with traditional media is their role in producing search results from generative AI. Large-language-model generative AI platforms, such as ChatGPT, Gemini, and Copilot, scour the internet to pull and aggregate existing information to form query responses. While there is some danger of hallucination, these AI platforms aren't attempting to invent information. Rather their goal is to pull valid information from credible sources. And what primary sources are they most frequently pulling from? Traditional news media.

For example, if you want to know if it's safe to eat at a restaurant chain after a reported outbreak of *E. coli*, you might search Google or ask ChatGPT about the chain's safety. In either case, AI will then scour what it's been taught are credible news sources. It's going to find, for example, what *The Washington Post* has said about the CDC's take on the outbreak, whether the company is claiming that the outbreak is under control as reported in *The Wall Street Journal*, and statistics on how long these types of outbreaks typically last as reported in the *Harvard Business Review*. Then, based on an analysis of the one hundred articles it's been able to review and aggregate in 0.23 seconds, AI will tell you whether it is likely or not that you're going to be OK eating at that restaurant chain.

If you're in charge of communications for that business and have decided that engaging with traditional media no longer makes sense, those outlets are going to write their stories about that *E. coli* outbreak anyway. And they're going to do it without including the restaurant chain's perspective. Since you haven't participated in the conversation, you end up at the mercy of those who have, and you can bet that your company's best insights are not part of the mix.

So in an ironic twist, if you don't engage with the old, you'll be left out of the new. Traditional media is both less relevant than it has ever been (in terms of primary audience) and yet vitally important as the information source populating the information interpretation engines of the future.

PLANNING EFFECTIVE MEDIA RELATIONS

The remainder of this chapter will focus on engaging with media effectively when you do choose to work with them.

TO ENGAGE OR NOT TO ENGAGE, THAT IS THE QUESTION

When the alarms are sounding, one of the most urgent demands of a crisis communicator is determining whether it's in your company's best interest to engage with the media at all around a particular matter. Discretion, or in this case, discernment, can truly be the better part of valor. Even if an issue affects your company deeply or you are chomping at the bit to advocate for a particular position, staying silent can be the right course of action. If you're on the fence about whether or not to weigh in on an issue, ask yourself first: Is this crisis even yours?

Often, when a major issue impacts an entire sector, reporters will seek out comments from companies they know will be most affected. For example, let's say the administration announces a tariff hike on aluminum. If you're in an industry that relies on imported aluminum in the manufacture of your products, this news is going to cause consequences up and down your supply chain. Your company is going to be scrambling for solutions to reduce the impact of these higher tariffs on your costs and, ultimately, on your customers.

Of course, you are not the only company in your industry dealing with the aluminum tariff fallout. But as a major player, it stands to reason that reporters who monitor the impact of tariff policy on business will come knocking at your door to get a reaction. You'll probably get an email, personalized to you and your company, from a respected reporter whose beat is your sector, seeking comment on whether and to what extent you're being impacted and how reactions to the tariff announcement are being handled internally.

Think carefully before crafting a response.

Even though it may look like the request is exclusive to you, there's a better-than-average chance that the reporter is casting a wide net throughout your industry, reaching out to similarly situated companies for their reactions as well.

In these instances, it's important to take a step back and think about whether there's truly any advantage to responding. What, exactly, would you be trying to accomplish by answering the reporter's request? Maybe this is an opportunity to rally the industry around a solution. Or maybe to clarify to investors how you are navigating the disruption. But if you don't have a clear goal in mind, you should take a pass. While you might be impacted by a particular change in law or policy shift, consider whether this is a crisis you need to address. It presents some internal issues to resolve, certainly, but every government action that has cost considerations doesn't require a personalized comment from you in the interest of crisis management. Instead, consider letting an industry spokesperson, a trade association representative, for example, address the impact from a holistic standpoint, and keep your company's internal machinations out of the fray.

In most cases, letting the pitch pass by won't diminish your reputation as a trusted source. Typically, the reporter reaching out to you for comment already has low expectations for a response to those kinds of requests. They've likely reached out to your competitors as well as the relevant industry spokespeople, knowing full well that most companies won't go out of their way to engage in matters that have little if any upside for them. They're playing a numbers game, reaching out to as many potential sources as possible, expecting to reel in a handful of reactions at best. Bottom line? If it's not your crisis, it's perfectly fine to sit it out.

If you determine that a certain situation does warrant media outreach, particularly if the crisis specifically involves your company, it's important to consider which reporters (or Substack authors, or influencers) are most likely to help you reach your objectives, including boosting your credibility.

TOUGH OVER FLUFF: CHOOSING CREDIBLE REPORTERS

This may seem counterintuitive, but in a crisis you don't always want to seek out the reporters you can count on to write a favorable story about your company. Often, it's better to engage with the person who's earned a reputation for fairness and accuracy, even if that means that your company might be raked over the coals from time to time. Toughness and credibility in reporting go hand in hand, and in a crisis, the most important ally you have is credibility. That's why if I need to engage on a tough issue, I rarely choose the friendliest reporter. Instead, I choose the reporter with a reputation for being fair while holding me or my client accountable.

If you're in the midst of a crisis and need to get your story out, find a journalist with a hard-hitting reputation. Seek out someone who understands your company and your industry and who will write the truth, even if it includes information about what your company missed. Your goal should be to make sure that the reporter understands what happened, how you are addressing the issue, and all of the remedial measures you're committed to undertaking in the future. It's true that this high level of authenticity and accuracy could result in a less flattering story, but the advantage is that you'll end up with a piece that engenders confidence in your company. If the outcome you're seeking is the restoration of trust, look for a journalist with an established reputation for being tough but fair.

Acclaimed *Seattle Times* aerospace reporter Dominic Gates never pulled any punches when it came to how he covered Boeing. He even won a Pulitzer Prize in 2020 for his coverage of the 737 MAX crisis, and you can believe that his reporting was thorough when it came to exposing Boeing's shortcomings and missteps. So, you might be surprised to learn that when I ran global media relations for the company, I'd often reach out to Dominic first when I had an important story to tell, especially if the story would impact the company's seventy thousand Washington-based workers.

I'd choose to go to Dominic for the simple reason that the people who mattered to the company, not to mention the folks who hand out the Pulitzers, trusted him. If Dominic Gates wrote the story, readers knew they were getting the unbiased truth.

REACH MEETS OBJECTIVES

When it comes to positioning your message, it's good to consider reach but always within the context of your broader objectives. For instance, *USA Today* has one of the highest circulations in the United States and beyond. Stories that appear in the publication have the potential to reach tens of millions of readers. But that doesn't mean *USA Today* is necessarily the best outlet for your message. If your company is in the tech sector for example, you might be much better off gaining coverage in *Wired*—where your message is assured of finding your core audience—than in a more widely distributed publication that has a general readership. If you have an issue that is of interest to a particular group, go for the outlet that best targets the people you want to reach rather than one that has the widest circulation.

But don't stop there. Think about the types of audiences different media outlets in your sector attract; the angle each journalist, commentator, or content creator is likely to take; and the types of questions you could be asked, and then plan your media strategy accordingly.

For a great example of how journalists in the same sector (in fact, on the same network) treat topics differently, look no further than Jim Cramer and Andrew Ross Sorkin, two well-known and respected anchors at CNBC who might approach the same story quite differently. Cramer, who hosts CNBC's *Mad Money* and co-anchors the station's *Squawk on the Street*, has a reputation for asking tough questions around how a certain company is or isn't acting in a way that drives value for shareholders. His subscription-based platform and shows are focused on information that's important to investors. He's all about what's driving the bottom line and whether and to what extent investors need to either shy away from or embrace a company based on its behavior.

Sorkin, a journalist with *The New York Times* who co-anchors CNBC's *Squawk Box*, takes a slightly different view. While he certainly focuses on bottom-line issues, he is also someone who likes to look at the bigger picture. Sorkin is more likely to ask questions about how your company treats its employees. Do you pay a living wage? What are the broader impacts of a situation or crisis when it comes to the environment and to society as a whole? When Sorkin examines the proliferation of generative AI, for example, he's more apt than Cramer to look beyond the technology's potential stock impact to examine issues such as the environmental impact of the big data centers needed to support the rapidly evolving technology.

So, if I am working communications for a client around a financial crisis—say the client is hitting a liquidity shortfall and people are afraid that the business is too bogged down in debt, and the firm's stock is starting to slip—I'll want to go on Jim Cramer's show because he's going to be open to my sharing the company's strategy and reasoning about how it's managing through the crisis. But if the same financial crisis has resulted in the threat of significant layoffs and I want to talk about an innovative new program that my client is rolling out to help stave off a workforce reduction, I'll likely want to go to Sorkin to talk about that. I have to be continuously evaluating these different personal approaches as I formulate my crisis communications strategy.

THE FALLACY THAT YOU CAN CONTROL THE MEDIA

There are some general rules to follow when dealing with the media. One is to try to avoid reporters who have demonstrated strong biases or predetermined points of view that are decidedly not in your favor. Remember, this happened to me when I engaged with the *New York Post* about communist spies. It's hard to get someone to course correct if the ship has already left the harbor. Another rule is to avoid falling into the "no comment" trap, as all you're doing is leaving a void for others to fill in, and what they're going to fill it in with is rarely going to be in your favor. And the third rule is that if you don't want to see it in print, don't say it.

That last one is easier said than done. In fact, it used to keep me up at night, until I faced down a situation that had the potential to tank my career.

FEAR FACTOR AND MEDIA MISSTEPS

One of my first high-stakes interviews with a reporter involved proprietary financial information. I was at Pratt & Whitney, and we had just sold part of the business to an international buyer. The deal was done, the strategy set, and now it was time to communicate. My job was to give an embargoed interview to *L'Echo*, the Belgian equivalent of *The*

Wall Street Journal. Even though I was apprehensive (read: shaking in my boots), I walked the reporter through the key points: the structure of the deal, the business model, and the mechanics.

After the interview, I debriefed with a business leader. His first question: "You didn't share the revenue numbers, did you?"

Panic hit me like a freight train. *Did I?* I rushed to my notes. I had. Worse, I had followed up with an email confirming the revenue number. I immediately tried calling the reporter to ask him not to use the number. No answer. I started sweating. I sent another email:

"Hey, I realized I may have given you a number that isn't completely accurate. I'm still verifying it. Can we talk?"

No response. An hour passed. Then two. The business executive followed up, "Did you clarify? Did you give him the number?" Legal started getting involved. I was convinced I'd just torpedoed my career.

The next morning, my worst fear came true. Not only did the reporter include the number in his story; he also put it in a pull quote. In bold. About as in-your-face as possible.

But by some weird twist of fate, it ultimately didn't matter.

For one, the article was in French. More importantly, it turned out that the number wasn't material at this level of the business. In other words, it was not big enough to have a substantive impact on our financials. Legal wasn't happy, but nothing actually changed. The story moved on. And so did we.

That mistake, early in my career, turned out to be liberating. It shattered the myth that you have to be perfect every time you talk to the press. No one is. The key is learning how to minimize mistakes that actually matter.

Looking back, that experience gave me confidence. It taught me that most of the time, a mistake isn't going to mean the end of the world. And once I realized that, I became a much better communicator.

But that doesn't mean I'd mastered the art of engaging the media. Later in my career, I'd learn that no matter how smart I thought I was, there was always the chance that a gifted reporter would end up outsmarting me in the end.

THE REPORTERS AS FRIENDS FALLACY

During the height of Boeing's 737 MAX crisis recovery efforts, as we worked to get planes back in the air, we wanted to prove that we had overhauled our production process to eliminate the quality issues that had plagued us. To do that, we invited Claire Bushey from the *Financial Times* to one of our production sites in Washington. The goal was simple: to show her, firsthand, the changes we had made, how they improved the production line, and why they gave confidence that such an issue wouldn't happen again.

Bringing in the *Financial Times* was a statement. This wasn't just a controlled rollout to a friendly audience or even a hard but local story for *The Seattle Times*; we were ready to show the world how far we'd come. So, we flew Claire out, and my team walked her through the facility, giving her rare access. Boeing had largely kept reporters at arm's length since the accidents, and she was one of the first to get meaningful time on the ground. It was a big deal.

Claire was engaged, professional, took in every presentation, and followed the tour closely. At one point, she excused herself to use the restroom. The team waited outside. She came back, and the group continued on.

Later that day, a female Boeing employee approached one of my colleagues. "Hey, I found these in the bathroom," she said, holding up a stack of business cards. They were all Claire's. Next to them was a note inviting employees to contact her anonymously.

She played her hand. The team would have been hard pressed to find those cards without help. What she hadn't counted on was getting outed so fast. I wasn't on the ground, but by all accounts, the rest of the visit was, understandably, awkward.

It was a reminder that reporters are there to do a job. Our interests and Claire's weren't the same. We wanted to show the world that we were fixing the problem. She was there to hold us accountable, to find the part we hadn't quite figured out yet. Sometimes, those objectives align. But you always have to assume a journalist will chase the most compelling angle for their readers.

To this day, I don't know how many people grabbed a card before we found them. And there wasn't much we could do about it. Sure, we could have confronted Claire and told her she abused our trust. But in the end, she did exactly what she was there to do. It's part of what makes her an excellent reporter. And I have no doubt that at least a few people reached out. Or, at the very least, put the card in their purses … just in case.

BEYOND EARNED MEDIA: OWNED MEDIA, PAY TO PLAY, AND MORE

Of course, not all coverage has to depend on a reporter's perceptions. If you're not leveraging owned media and paid options, you're missing out on opportunities to get your message out quickly and accurately. In fact, with consumers becoming increasingly media agnostic, meaning they care less about where their information comes from than how it can be accessed,[60] you'll be missing a key component of

60 Nic Newman, "Overview and Key Findings of the 2025 Digital News Report," Reuters Institute, June 17, 2025, https://reutersinstitute.politics.ox.ac.uk/digital-news-report/2025/dnr-executive-summary.

brand management if you're not leveraging owned and paid media to your messaging advantage.

Owned media, including your website, blogs, newsletters, social media pages, and self-produced podcasts, are your lowest-hanging fruit. When you publish a statement on your website, you reduce the likelihood that you'll be misquoted or that your messaging will be misconstrued. You can publish new information as it occurs and then push it out on all of your owned channels, ensuring that your core constituents—your followers and the news media that cover your industry—receive timely and accurate information.

Paid outlets, including pay-to-play awards, sponsored content, and advertorials, also have their place in your branding mix. The more avenues your messages flow through and the more consistent the messages are, the greater the likelihood you'll gain the traction you're seeking and that influencers will pick up the story and retell it from your point of view.

THE ROBBY STARBUCK MODEL

I can't conclude a chapter on the modern media gauntlet without acknowledging the unadulterated success of conservative media influencer Robby Starbuck. No matter how you feel about him, Starbuck has cracked the code on how to leverage every available media-related tool to get a message across and reach desired outcomes.

After a successful career as a music video director and music-related influencer on Myspace, Starbuck burst onto the political scene during the pandemic years, amassing conservative followers as he cut his conservative influencer teeth on issues such as opposing mask and vaccine mandates. As his online profile grew, Starbuck perfected the art of leveraging both new media platforms and traditional outlets to achieve his desired outcomes.

Specifically, Starbuck's modus operandi is to go directly to the pages and profiles of corporate executives and offer them ultimatums. *End that DEI program or face the wrath of my network!* If the company acquiesces, he declares victory to his base. If not, he rallies his followers, both human and bots on autopilot, to join his crusade by flooding the targeted page with vitriol. Bolstering these efforts by posting video content on X, Instagram, and Facebook has gotten him and his causes online momentum, but he still makes a specific effort to cultivate traditional coverage in traditional media outlets, such as *Bloomberg*, *Fortune*, and *Yahoo! News*, to legitimize his platform. His strategy of sowing seeds of disruption across platforms and paradigms has paid off, as several well-known companies are said to have altered or eliminated their DEI policies after Starbucks targeted them.

The companies that thrive in crisis aren't the ones playing defense; they're the ones smart enough to master both the credibility of traditional media and the reach of new platforms.

Love it or hate it, the Robby Starbuck model represents something bigger than just one influencer's playbook. It's proof that the old rules of media engagement are dead, and the new ones reward those bold enough to use every tool in the arsenal. While Starbuck's tactics may feel extreme, his success illustrates a fundamental truth: In today's fractured media landscape, either *you* control your narrative or someone else will. The companies that thrive in crisis aren't the ones playing defense; they're the ones smart enough to master both the credibility of traditional media and the reach of new platforms. That's not just a good communications strategy. That's survival.

Key Learnings:

- Traditional media still validates, but new media amplifies.
- Choose tough reporters over friendly ones in a crisis.
- Not every crisis that impacts you is your cross to bear.
- The no-comment trap leaves voids others will fill.
- The most effective communications strategies integrate new and traditional media seamlessly, with a clear goal to ground it all.

All of these lessons remain true whether your audience is investors or employees, though employees come with their own unique set of considerations.

CHAPTER SEVEN

EMPLOYEE IDENTITY

RECONCILING EMPLOYEE–EMPLOYER EXPECTATIONS

The competition for talent has never been more brutal or more confusing. Meta has made offers worth over $1 billion to poach top AI researchers. Companies are clawing back control with return-to-office mandates that have employees dusting off their resumes. The mutual loyalty that once defined the employee–employer relationship? Dead and buried with the pension plans of the 1990s.

Employees demand purpose, flexibility, and alignment with their values, and they'll jump ship the moment those expectations aren't met. Employers, meanwhile, are dealing with talent that costs more, expects more, and sticks around less. Job cuts across every industry have ratcheted up the pressure on both sides. Everyone's hedging their bets. Everyone's looking over their shoulders.

Welcome to the new employee–employer social contract: a high-stakes game in which neither side quite trusts the other. There is a tendency in corporate America to think about the workforce in terms of productivity. It's easy to measure the value of an employee through metrics such as units produced, tasks completed, sales closed, revenue generated, or hours billed. Setting and achieving key performance indicators is undoubtedly important in keeping your business competitive. But it's also important to understand that an employee's value encompasses more than how many parts they can install in a certain time frame or how many sales they can close in a quarter. Your employees have the potential to be your greatest brand ambassadors. But they can also be your biggest detractors.

In many ways, your employees are your most important stakeholders. They are the people with the most skin in the game when it comes to rooting for your success. If you haven't captured the hearts and minds of the people working closest with you, then you can be certain that you'll have a tough time holding on to the loyalty of your other stakeholders, such as customers and investors, should you face a crisis or a negative event.

Helping corporations to understand and enhance their relationships with their employees is such a vital part of what my colleagues and I do as comms consultants that BPI regularly conducts field surveys on employee sentiment.[61] It probably won't surprise you that our findings consistently show that in the post-pandemic work world, employees largely feel disconnected from their employers.

The complaints may sound familiar. Workers don't understand the organization's purpose, perhaps because they also report that no one bothers to share the leadership's vision with them. Since they don't have access to the big picture, they don't understand the role they could be playing in achieving the organization's broader goals.

---

61 Bradley Akubuiro, "The Surprising Thing Your Employees Still Believe. And How Better Communications Can Help," *Inc.*, December 10, 2023, https://www.inc.com/bradley-akubuiro/the-surprising-thing-your-employees-still-believe-how-better-communications-can-help.html..

But here's the kicker. Many employees say they would consider taking a fairly large pay cut just to work for a company that they feel aligned with, and which they think will treat them with greater regard. Not only does a lack of communication with your workforce add to their discontent, but it also means they won't hesitate to abandon ship for a workplace where management seems more empowering and forthcoming, even if it means less money.

It's clear that if you want your biggest stakeholders to have your back, you're going to have to find ways to provide them with the lived experience of being a part of something greater than themselves.

THE BACKYARD BARBECUE TEST

In the pressure to keep a business moving forward, it can be easy to forget that every worker who shows up for your company daily is an individual, an autonomous and complex human being with their own personal needs and desires, hopes and dreams, thoughts and fears. The best business leaders know that you get the best out of employees when you recognize and honor their individuality. Great leaders look beyond outcomes and take the time to understand that what a person does and where they work forms a huge part of their identity. And, as a leader, you want that identity to manifest in a way that reflects positively on your business. In turn, you want your company to be a positive force in your employees' lives.

So how can you gauge how your employees feel about your company? One way is to find out how they talk about their job to strangers. BPI's founder, Andrew Bleeker, and I like to call this the backyard barbecue test (or the cocktail party test, depending on your audience).

Here's the gist. Your employee meets someone new at a neighborhood barbecue. The goal is to understand how many questions it takes for a stranger to find out that this individual works for your company. You also want to find out how they couch that association. Look at how many layers of questions and answers it takes for them to specify that they work for you, then see how they describe the experience. The more layers, the less they identify with the job and the company. The fewer the layers, the more positive they are to feel about the company and their role in its success.

So, if one of your employees were asked, "What do you do?" and their response was, "I work in tech," that would be one layer. If they're asked again and respond with something like, "I work in data security," that's two layers. If it takes a third probe for the employee to say, "I work at Data Gurus International," that's a signal that the employee doesn't strongly identify with your company or that something about the organization feels incongruent with their personal identity right now. If there were no disconnect, it wouldn't take three layers of questions to get there; someone might instead say, "I work in product design at Apple. I get to help make the products we love to use more elegant and user-friendly."

You're not going to get this level of enthusiastic response from everyone, and that's OK. But if it consistently takes three or four questions to get an employee to mention their affiliation with your company, it's worth examining why. The goal is to turn employees into advocates, in good times and bad.

LEADING WITH YOUR HUMANITY

When tragedy strikes or a crisis occurs, you're going to need your employees to have your back. If you haven't already earned the loyalty of the people closest to your enterprise and its mission, winning over your other stakeholders, not to mention the public, will be an even steeper uphill battle.

I'll never forget walking the shop floor at Pratt & Whitney for the first time almost two decades ago and seeing the machinists, many of whom had worked for the company for twenty or thirty years, proudly sporting arm tattoos of the company's eagle logo. What an amazing way to show their allegiance to the company that had been such a significant part of their lives! These were proud and loyal members of the Pratt & Whitney family, and I've always been amazed that they were willing to show that loyalty in such an overt and permanent way.

While many companies today try to promote a sense of belonging by focusing efforts on culture and community, it's doubtful they'll bring back the kind of pride in a profession that compels a person to brand their bodies with the symbol of their employer. To the machinists, the eagle tattoos were a tangible manifestation of the grit and determination it takes to produce powerful, precision-engineered airplane engines.

So, what can you do to create an environment where your workforce has your back? The answer is to treat your employees like the critical stakeholders that they are. And that begins with showing your human side consistently and authentically. Whether you have one hundred employees or one hundred thousand, when it comes to managing through a crisis—especially when the crisis impacts your workers—it's more important than ever to put a human face on leadership.

Zoom CEO Models Accountability

Zoom CEO Eric Yuan understood this when he informed his employees via email in February 2023 that the company would be laying off 1,300 workers worldwide. While the fact that the company would be reducing its workforce wasn't exactly a shock, as Q1 2023 was a particularly difficult time in the tech space, it was remarkable that Yuan directly assumed accountability for the company's challenges.

"We didn't take as much time as we should have to thoroughly analyze our teams or assess if we were growing sustainably, toward the highest priorities," he said in the email. "As the CEO and founder of Zoom, I am accountable for these mistakes and the actions we take today … To that end, I am reducing my salary for the coming fiscal year by 98 percent and foregoing my FY23 corporate bonus."[62]

It would have been easy for Yuan to blame market conditions and forces outside of his control for the company's setbacks, but instead, he put the blame on himself and the leadership, noting that other members of his executive team would see significant base salary reductions and forfeit bonuses. By owning his mistakes and making a commitment to do better in the future, Yuan succeeded in helping his remaining employees feel safer and more connected to the company as it moved through the crisis, while perhaps softening the blow for those he had to let go.

Trust Wins Hearts and Minds

Whether it's a layoff or another type of crisis, it's difficult to work your way through a solemn situation without your work community on your side. In later chapters, I'll be focusing on the mechanics of preparing for a possible crisis and managing your way through all kinds of sticky situations. As you're reviewing that information, I

62 Bradley Akubuiro, "What President Zelensky and the CEO of Zoom Both Understand About the Power of Symbolism," *Inc.*, March 3, 2023, https://www.inc.com/bradley-akubuiro/what-president-zelensky-ceo-of-zoom-both-understand-about-power-of-symbolism.html.

encourage you to keep the effect your behavior has on your employees top of mind by continually asking yourself the following:

- How do our employees think and feel about what we're doing? Is their perception that we are taking the necessary steps to protect the public, the business, and them?
- Do our employees understand our challenges and feel like they are part of the solution?
- Do our employees feel like they are better off for being associated with this company than they would have been if they were not associated with it?
- Do our employees feel like management is being transparent with them about what's going on?

Pay particular attention to that last question. Because when you get right down to it, loyalty is all about trust. And trust is, by definition, always a two-way street.

TWO-WAY TRUST AND RADICAL TRANSPARENCY

Sometimes, a culture of secrecy doesn't just breed leaks; it creates crusaders. At Theranos, Elizabeth Holmes built a fortress of nondisclosure agreements, compartmentalized information, and legal intimidation designed to keep employees from talking. The company's blood-testing technology was supposedly revolutionary, but employees working on different pieces of the puzzle weren't allowed to compare notes or ask questions about the bigger picture. When lab technician Tyler Shultz raised concerns about inaccurate test results, he was isolated and threatened with lawsuits rather than engaged in honest dialogue about patient safety.[63]

The paranoid culture backfired spectacularly. Shultz didn't just leak to a reporter; he became a federal whistleblower who helped bring down the entire company. Because leadership had created an environment where legitimate concerns were treated as acts of betrayal, Shultz felt his only option was to go outside the company entirely. What started as internal quality control questions became a *Wall Street Journal* investigation that exposed systemic fraud. Holmes's obsession with controlling information transformed a concerned employee into the primary witness in her own criminal prosecution. The very secrecy meant to protect Theranos became the weapon that destroyed it.[64]

Caitlin Hayden, who leads communications at BAE Systems, believes that engendering trust that goes both ways is essential to building a functioning culture. We talk often about these concepts, and recently, she explained her belief that radical transparency will always win the day. According to Caitlin, if you treat employees as the adults that they are, you will be rewarded with both their trust and their respect.

Caitlin had occasion to test this thesis in a high-stakes situation not too long before we spoke. BAE maintains operations around the world. One of its facilities is in a country that had recently become embroiled in a wave of terrorist activity, which was quickly devolving into a regional ground war. BAE leadership was completely forthcoming with its worldwide staff about the potential impact and

63 Lauren Rogal, "Secrets, Lies, and Lessons from the Theranos Scandal," *UC Law Journal* 72, no. 6 (2021): 1663–1702, https://repository.uclawsf.edu/hastings_law_journal/vol72/iss6/3.

64 "Theranos Whistleblower Shares His Story," Boston College Carroll School of Management, Spring 2020, https://www.bc.edu/bc-web/schools/carroll-school/sites/winston-center/newsletter/newsletter-archive/Spring-2020/forum-on-business-ethics-s2020update.html.

the company's future strategy despite the volatility of the situation. Importantly, BAE communicated the reasons behind these decisions. The company made it clear that the information it was imparting was confidential and needed to remain so, and amazingly, not one of the company's one hundred thousand employees broke the confidence they had been entrusted with. Without exception, each member of the BAE global workforce understood the stakes and stepped up to the plate to protect their colleagues and BAE's interests.

Caitlin explained that the key to establishing this level of mutual trust comes from sharing the why behind decisions.

"We need to treat our employees like grown-ups and not have a parent–child relationship where we don't tell them things because we can't trust them," she said. "People may not like a decision, but if they feel you've told them the truth and explained why you made it, they often say, 'I get it.' It's when people feel they weren't heard that stray voltage happens."

Building this kind of radical transparency also requires being open to discussing both problems and successes openly and honestly, something Allison England, head of US & Canada Communications at GE HealthCare, embraces wholeheartedly. In fact, in GE HealthCare's communications culture, this is referred to as "embracing the reds."

As Allison, who also happens to be my wife, explains it, this approach encourages employees to surface concerns rather than hide them, and it gives leadership a chance to respond in kind. "We talk about embracing the reds. The more openly you talk about the things that are not going well and the things that are with the same tone, the more willing your people will be to bring forward matters they're concerned about to you. It all becomes part of the process."

BUILDING A FOUNDATION OF TRUST, ONE INTERACTION AT A TIME

At the beginning of this chapter, I talked about how important it is for leadership to recognize that each employee is a unique and complex human being. It's equally important for us to put a human face on leadership, to show the humanity and compassion that goes into the decisions your company makes, especially as it faces a crisis.

I agree with my friend Sara Fletcher, vice president of corporate affairs for Oatly, who argues that there is no holding back when it comes to how real you're going to be with your employees. Sara says that employee buy-in *requires* genuine dialogue. Authentic conversation, she says, becomes essential for maintaining internal alignment, especially when employees disagree with a company's position.

"The best answer is as much rationale and human real talk as possible, human to human, not comms to employees. It's important to have a party line, but if that's all an employee is given, and especially if they don't agree with it, getting them to be a brand advocate or comfortable with a decision is next to impossible."

It's important to find ways for your top brass to communicate with the rank and file directly. Whether it's through town hall meetings, video or audio conferencing, prerecorded videos, or written missives, make sure leadership speaks from a place of authenticity, transparency, and compassion.

Sometimes, it will take a good amount of work and even coaching to get your top executive comfortable with the role of comforter-in-chief. But it's necessary, especially during a crisis. Everyone is watching for leadership's cues. Everyone is looking to leadership for strength and solace. Create the space to let that happen.

In my experience working with organizations during times of immense chaos and crisis, when you bring your entire company into the fold, two things happen. Everyone feels like a part of the solution, which in itself can be healing. And you'll find that the people closest to the ground are the ones who often come up with the best solutions. The adage "never waste a good crisis" also means never passing up the opportunity to learn from your biggest stakeholders: your employees, who, if you nurture the relationship, will always have your back.

Key Learnings:

- Employees can be your greatest ambassadors or your biggest detractors.
- Understand employee identity and view employees not just as a subservient monolith but rather as an audience to be courted.

Ask yourself this: How will you ensure that employees view themselves as better off from their association with your organization than they would have been without it?

INTERLUDE

CHAPTER EIGHT

BEFORE THE STORM

HOW TO AVOID LOSING THE CRISIS BEFORE IT STARTS

In 2011, I sat in the back seat of a government sedan cutting through the chaotic streets of Monrovia, Liberia. I was there at the invitation of President Ellen Johnson Sirleaf, tasked with building Liberia's national leadership development program and corresponding government policy. Liberia had lost most of its institutional capacity during a fourteen-year civil war. I was now on my way to a meeting with some of the country's highest-ranking officials to discuss the path forward.

As the car traversed the city streets, we passed homes and buildings littered with bullet holes—sobering reminders of the freshness of this country's conflict. I paid little attention to the incessant honking as battered minibuses, bright yellow taxis, motorbikes, and cars competed for the right of way or swerved to avoid hitting street vendors hawking everything from bananas to prepaid phone cards. My focus, instead, was on the government document I'd just been handed. It was related to my assignment. At one point, I came to this sentence: "The vast majority of the country's top leaders and potential leaders were either killed or driven out by the threat of death."

I put the paper down and took that in. Liberia's entire leadership infrastructure had collapsed, and the president wanted me to help lay the groundwork for reestablishing it. To say that this felt like an impossible task would be an understatement. It felt like being asked to rebuild a house from rubble with my bare hands. I picked up the document again and continued reading. There were leadership organizations in Liberia that had survived despite the chaos and turmoil that had engulfed the country's political infrastructure for years. We wouldn't be starting from zero.

As I dug deeper, I learned that these surviving organizations had three things in common. They each had held on to clear principles that they followed rigorously. They each maintained the same strong relationships across government, funders, experts, and communities that they had forged before war broke out. And they each incorporated simple decision-making structures that worked even when every other kind of structure—physical, political, administrative—seemed to have slipped away.

The task ahead began to seem a bit less daunting. I realized that when systems break down, you don't need complex policies and procedures to build them up again. Instead, you need solid frameworks that help people make good decisions under bad circumstances. In other words, organizations that survive crises, even civil war, stick to a simple three-pronged framework:

- Know where you stand and stand there, a topic I discussed in detail in chapter 5.
- Create a strong infrastructure that prepares you to withstand any crisis.

- Leverage your principles and your established infrastructure to see you through the crisis.

To this day, this framework continues to inform my own moves as a crisis communications professional, beginning with how I advise corporate leadership to prepare for crisis situations.

BUILDING A FOUNDATION FOR CRISIS MANAGEMENT

The best crisis management is prevention. Stop the fire before it starts. But since that isn't always possible, the most effective way to survive a crisis is to prepare a strong crisis management and communications infrastructure well before a crisis hits. If you accomplish this first phase of crisis management, the preparation phase, you'll find that the next two phases—managing through a crisis and postcrisis improvement, discussed in later chapters—will be much easier to handle.

The goal of crisis preparation is to turn potential disasters into manageable challenges. Organizations that prepare well don't just survive their crises; they often emerge stronger than before. They build deeper stakeholder trust, clearer internal processes, and more resilient cultures. The companies that try to wing it, that assume they can figure it out when the time comes, don't just fail in their crisis response; they often don't survive the crisis at all.

I'm not saying that you can scenario plan for every event or circumstance that will cross your path or affect your company. But you can build capabilities to handle almost anything that comes your way. You can develop relationships that become lifelines during and after a crisis. You can practice decision-making so that making the right call in a high-stress situation becomes instinct. You can lay the foundation you'll need to protect your organization from both the expected and the unexpected.

Think of this chapter as the blueprint for building a crisis-proof foundation, one that won't crumble when the ground starts to shake. Because here's the thing: Crisis isn't a matter of if, but when. And when it hits, you'll either be ready or you'll be roadkill.

WHAT IS A CRISIS?

I define a true crisis as an unexpected event that threatens your ability to operate, your reputation, or the safety of people who depend on you.

Not every bad headline is a crisis, and not every warning is a false alarm. I've seen companies mobilize like they're fighting World War III over a bad tweet that would have blown over in forty-eight hours. I've also watched CEOs ignore flashing red lights until their entire business got blown up around them.

So how do you determine what actually constitutes a crisis? I define a true crisis as an unexpected event that threatens your ability to operate, your reputation, or the safety of people who depend on you. But take note! The operative term here is *threatens*, not "annoys," "complicates," or "creates some bad press."

Distinguishing a Crisis from an Issue

Here's where most leaders get it wrong: They either panic at every hiccup or sleepwalk through real disasters.

As someone who cut her teeth managing issues across multiple continents for the US State Department, BAE's Caitlin Hayden puts it perfectly: "Almost nothing is a crisis now. It's gotta be really serious to be a crisis. Unless it's threatening our license to operate, we don't need crisis mode."

The Crisis Test: Four Questions

If you're wondering if an incident or situation has risen to the level of a true crisis, ask yourself these four questions:

1. **Are you under real-time pressure**? Do you need to make decisions in hours, not days?
2. **Is there potential for significant stakeholder impact**? Could this materially harm people who trust you?
3. **Is this something that will garner significant public attention**? Will this attract media coverage or social media amplification?
4. **Is there a real threat to operations**? Could this disrupt your core business or change how you're regulated?

If three out of four are yes, congratulations, you're officially in crisis mode. If it's fewer than three, you're probably dealing with an issue that needs some serious management but not crisis-level resources.

I don't mean to diminish the importance of addressing critical issues quickly and decisively, especially those that could turn into crises if not properly addressed. Issues are important, certainly, but they are more easily managed than crises.

Characteristics of an Issue

You're dealing with an issue if the following are true:

- **You have time to think**. You can deliberate, get input, and plan properly.

- **The impact is contained**. The issue doesn't threaten your fundamental operations.
- **You can address it with standard processes**. Your normal business workflows can handle the situation.
- **The matter is delegable**. Middle management can lead the response.

The Gray Zone: When Issues Become Crises

So, what transforms a manageable issue into a full-blown crisis?

- **Volume and velocity**: when the conversation about your company spikes dramatically in a short window
- **Audience expansion**: when the people talking aren't just your usual critics
- **Narrative crystallization**: when a simple, damaging story about you starts spreading
- **Stakeholder attention**: when people with real power over your business start asking questions

The companies that are adept at managing the gray zone have early warning systems. They're monitoring not just what's being said but who's saying it, how fast it's spreading, and whether it's reaching audiences that actually matter to their business. And they have a crisis plan at the ready in the event the issue devolves into a crisis.

Crisis Dimensions: Understanding the Battlefield

Before you can prepare for a crisis, let alone manage it, you need to understand where the battles are going to be fought. And that means you need to understand the situation across four dimensions: the scope of the crisis, who the stakeholders are, what the timeline is, and whether and to what extent the crisis was predictable.

PREPARING FOR A CRISIS: A SIX-STEP FRAMEWORK

Katie Hill, senior vice president of communications at the NFL and a former communications leader in the Obama administration, learned the importance of crisis preparation during her White House days and applied it early in her time at the NFL. "Having good processes in place before a crisis hits matters most. Being nimble, being transparent, not being afraid to say difficult things out loud, including when you don't know things. That garnered credibility with journalists, fans, and teams."

Bingo. Having good processes in place well before a crisis hits is absolutely necessary if you're going to successfully manage through whatever predicament you find yourself in. And establishing and maintaining credibility is the natural result of solid preparation. After working in the trenches with top communications pros such as Katie for nearly two decades, I've distilled comprehensive crisis prep into the following six-step framework.

Step 1: Evaluate Risks (Know Your Vulnerabilities)

There is no substitute here for brutal honesty. You'll need to take a good, hard look at both internal and external factors that could play a role in propelling your company into crisis mode. I'm not talking about the measured risks you talk about in management meetings, such as standard fluctuations in your stock price, but the serious stuff that keeps you up at night.

Use the following attack surface assessment to help with identifying and evaluating risks.

Attack Surface Assessment

Internal Risks

- Operational failures: plant accidents, system crashes, supply chain breaks
- People problems: leadership scandals, employee misconduct, whistleblower allegations
- Product issues: safety defects, quality failures, cyber vulnerabilities
- Financial exposure: fraud, accounting irregularities, major client losses

External Risks

- Market disruption: competitor moves, regulatory changes, economic shocks
- Natural disasters: weather events, pandemics, infrastructure failures
- Social/political shifts: culture war targeting, activist campaigns, policy changes
- Third-party failures: vendor problems, partner scandals, industry-wide issues

The goal in this step isn't to catalog every possible risk. Rather, it's to identify the five to seven scenarios most likely to threaten your business model.

Step 2: Assemble a Crisis Response Team, a.k.a. Your Crisis War Cabinet

One of the biggest mistakes I see companies make is that they build their crisis teams as if they were putting together a conference call. They call on twenty people, representing every possible constituency in their organization, to attend a mandatory meeting to "align on messaging."

That's not a crisis team; that's a committee. And committees have no place in the war room.

Dana Salloum's approach as CCO at Alstom exemplifies this principle in action. Operating across more than sixty countries, her team has refined crisis response into a surgical process that balances speed with accuracy.

"When a potential crisis surfaces, we stand up a crisis cell, which is a small, cross-functional group from the relevant country, region, and HQ to gather facts, assess the severity, and decide next steps," Salloum explains. "The aim is speed, accuracy, and alignment from the start."

Assemble a Small but Mighty Team

Like the crisis cells employed at Alstom, your core crisis response team should be small and powerful. It should also be available 24/7. Think SEAL Team Six, not company picnic planning committee. Start by choosing your five core team members:

- **Choose a crisis leader**. This doesn't have to be the CEO, but it does have to be someone with real authority. This person must be able to make a fast and actionable decision when it matters most.

- **Bring in someone from operations**. Make sure this person is both in the weeds of how your facilities work and has the wherewithal to actually stop the bleeding operationally.
- **Tap a communications guru**. This must be someone who can be the voice of the company and speak on its behalf publicly, such as an internal spokesperson or a trusted outside consultant.
- **Include a legal advisor**. When selecting legal counsel, make sure you find someone who understands both the law as it applies to your business and the business realities and repercussions of any proposed actions (or nonactions).
- **Bring in people management**. This person must bring expertise in both employee relations and crisis dynamics to act as your team's HR leader.

This core team consists of the people who will come to the company's aid at the drop of a hat, no matter what. These are your ride or dies. They'll be your greatest allies when planning strategy, and they'll be in the thick of things during execution. But they aren't the whole team. You're going to need to tap into different areas of expertise, depending on the nature of the crisis. It's important to choose an extended team to be ready when you need them. Members might include representatives from the following functions within your organization:

- **Government relations**: for crises involving regulatory or policy issues or societal matters that could have political undertones
- **Investor relations**: if you're a public company or are at risk of major financial exposures
- **Security/IT**: for cyber, physical safety, or technology-related crises

- **Customer service**: to address consumer-facing problems
- **Finance**: for assistance with business continuity and resource decisions

While they don't have to be at every meeting, these extended team members should be on speed dial—ready, willing, and able to lend their expertise as needed. And your issue set may dictate that colleagues from the second category be moved to the core team. Personally, I always aim to stay in lockstep with investor relations. I've gotten so deep in their world that I teach a master's degree course on investor relations at Northwestern.

To be effective, your crisis response structure and crew must meet certain essential (and nonnegotiable) criteria:

- **The team stays lean and mean**. Make sure your core team never exceeds seven people. Any more than that, and you'll have too many layers to be effective.
- **Every team member must be empowered to make decisions**. In a crisis, time is of the essence, and nobody can wait for sign-offs from superiors. Autonomy must be nonnegotiable.
- **Everyone is on call, always**. I'm talking 24/7 availability when the shit hits the fan. That means everyone provides their contact info, backup contacts, and backup plans for the backup contacts.
- **You trust each other**. You don't want to start establishing credibility among the team when you're deep in a situation that requires hard decisions and immediate execution. Try to choose individuals who know one another, respect each other, and have worked together before under pressure.

Step 3: Instead of a Crisis Playbook, Build a CPS (Crisis Positioning System)

Your crisis playbook shouldn't look like a federal regulation—thick, unreadable, and ignored when it matters most. I've seen too many companies create two-hundred-page documents that collect dust until someone's career is on the line at 2:00 a.m. Your playbook needs to be practical, accessible, and built for people making decisions under pressure when stakes are highest.

The core of an effective playbook—exclusive of templates and contact lists—should be no more than fifteen pages. It needs clear guidelines, identified vulnerabilities, and actionable filters that work in real time. Think: *Under attack? Spread the pressure.* Pressure equals force divided by surface area. Your attackers will try to concentrate fire on a single point. Your job is to disperse it.

The Essential Foundation

Before you can build something better, you need the basics:

- **Crisis Classification**—Type (operational, reputational, regulatory, financial), scope (local to global), timeline (hours, days, or months), and stakeholder impact.
- **Decision Authority**—Use RACI: who's Responsible for execution, who's Accountable for final calls, who gets Consulted, who stays Informed. Authority must be clear before the crisis hits.
- **Communication Protocols**—Internal notification sequences, external approval chains, stakeholder contact databases (updated quarterly), and channel management for different audiences.

- **Template Library**—Pre-drafted, legally reviewed holding statements for common scenarios. In a crisis, you'll have thirty minutes or less before the media writes the story without you. Holding statements buy you time precisely when time isn't on your side.

This is table stakes. But here's the problem: Even the best static playbook can't keep pace with the speed and complexity of modern crisis.

Enter the Crisis Positioning System

Think GPS, but for reputation risk.

A GPS doesn't just give you a map and wish you luck. It tracks your position in real time, reroutes when conditions change, learns from traffic patterns, and adapts continuously. That's what modern crisis management requires—and that's what a Crisis Positioning System (CPS) delivers.

CPS replaces your static playbook with a living, learning architecture. It's designed to help you sense threats early, decide intelligently, act fast, and adapt continuously using both machine intelligence and human judgment. Here's how it works:

1. Inputs—Sense the Terrain

CPS constantly monitors live data streams: media and social sentiment, internal employee signals, regulatory activity, competitive intelligence. AI flags anomalies, pattern-matches against historic crises, and ranks vulnerabilities by business impact. It's your early-warning radar—a crisis weather system that shows storms forming before they hit.

2. Interpretation—Fix Your Position

AI clusters signals into scenarios and cross-references them with your vulnerability library—your known weak spots, controversial partnerships, DEI flashpoints, litigation risks. It pulls relevant past statements, Q&As, and holding lines to show what precedent you've already set. It gives you confidence scores on what's verified versus volatile. The system tells you not just what's happening, but how exposed you are.

3. Response—Plot the Route

This is where CPS becomes a command center. You upload draft responses, and AI models stakeholder reactions—employees, customers, investors, policymakers—using learned personas. It tailors messages in each executive's voice based on prior communications. It scours your list of regular reporters and influencers to propose those most critical to reach proactively. All historical materials become modular and auto-update to match new context. Leaders still decide, but CPS shortens the distance from awareness to action.

4. Recalibration—Reroute in Real Time

As messages go live, CPS tracks response patterns, identifies sentiment shifts, flags contradictions. It auto-suggests pivots: "Policymaker tone trending negative on 'innovation' framing—recommend emphasizing 'safety' instead." Every interaction makes the system smarter and your responses more precise.

5. Output—The Learning Loop

CPS doesn't close files—it builds institutional memory. It stores crisis-response data, stakeholder reaction patterns, and post-crisis diagnostics. What worked? What failed? What improved trust metrics? The system continuously retrains AI to refine future detection and messaging. Your organization becomes progressively more crisis-resilient—not by adding more rules, but because your system keeps learning.

The Bottom Line

Throw out your crisis playbook. Build a Crisis Positioning System—an AI-enabled framework that knows your vulnerabilities, learns your voice, anticipates stakeholder reactions, and guides you through the storm in real time. Because in a world moving at the speed of social media, static documents don't save reputations. Dynamic systems do.

Template Inputs for CPS Knowledge Base

The following should be pre-drafted, legally reviewed, and ready to customize:

Holding Statements for Common Scenarios

Holding statements are your crisis insurance policies. In a crisis, you'll typically have thirty minutes or less to respond to the media before they write the story without you. Your holding statement is used as a placeholder to acknowledge the issue and demonstrate that you're working hard to address the situation. Holding statements buy you time precisely when time is not on your side.

DEVELOPING EFFECTIVE HOLDING STATEMENTS: YOUR FIRST RESPONSE ARSENAL

A holding statement is your crisis team's equivalent of a first aid kit: You hope you never need it, but when you do, you need it to work perfectly and immediately.

Raj Shah, who served as deputy White House press secretary under President Trump and later as deputy chief of staff to Speaker Mike Johnson, puts it bluntly: "The timeliness of information is just as important as the effectiveness of it. If it's a day late, it's no longer relevant. Companies have a tendency to be slow."

The Three-Part Framework That Actually Works

Part 1: Acknowledge the Situation (Facts Only)

State what you know to be true, nothing more.

- When: "We became aware at [time] that …"
- What: "An incident occurred involving …"
- Where: "At our [location] facility …"
- Avoid speculation: Don't guess about causes, impacts, or outcomes.

Part 2: Show Genuine Concern (Human Connection)

This isn't corporate speak; it's human emotion.

- **Prioritize people**. "The safety and well-being of our [employees/customers/community] is our first concern."
- **Acknowledge impact.** "We understand this is concerning for …"
- **Express authentic emotion.** Use words such as "deeply concerned" or "taking this seriously."

Part 3: Demonstrate Action (What You're Actually Doing)

Give people confidence that you have the situation under control.

- **Immediate response**: "We have immediately …"
- **Investigation commitment**: "We are working with [authorities/experts] to understand …"

- **Communication promise**: "We will provide updates as more information becomes available."
- **Contact information**: "For questions, please contact …"

Ready-to-Deploy Holding Statements

General crisis template: "We are aware of the [type of incident] that occurred at [location/time]. Our team is currently assessing the situation and will provide updates as more information becomes available. The well-being of our [customers/employees/community] is our foremost concern. For inquiries, please contact [contact information]."

Safety incident template: "We are deeply concerned about the [safety incident] that occurred at our [location] facility [time]. Our first priority is the safety and well-being of our employees and community. We are working closely with [emergency responders/authorities] and have [specific action taken]. We will provide updates as our investigation progresses."

Data security template: "We recently discovered [type of security incident] that may have affected [type] information. We immediately secured our systems and are investigating the extent of the incident. We are working with cybersecurity experts and law enforcement as appropriate. We will notify affected individuals directly and provide regular updates."

Product issue template: "We have received reports of [product issue] with [product name]. Customer safety is our top priority, and we are immediately [specific action]. As a precautionary measure, we recommend [customer action]. We are working to understand the scope and will provide additional guidance as soon as possible."

The Dos and Don'ts That Matter

Dos

- Keep it under 150 words; people won't read more in a crisis.
- Use active voice and clear language that your grandmother would understand.
- Include specific next steps and contact information.
- Have legal review templates in advance, not during the crisis. Agree early on the balance between humanity and liability in language.
- Update templates quarterly based on new scenarios.

Don'ts

- Assign blame or accept responsibility prematurely.
- Make promises you can't keep ("We guarantee this will never happen again").
- Use corporate jargon or technical language.
- Downplay the situation or sound defensive.
- Provide unverified information just to fill the silence.

Remember: **A holding statement buys you time to get the real story right**. It's not your final word; it's your first responsible word.

Internal Communications Templates for Employees

How and when you talk to your people when things go sideways can make or break your employees' perception of your company. As I talked about in chapter 7, your employees can be your greatest advocates or your biggest detractors. Pre-plan what you're going to say to your staff before a crisis hits, then tweak and deploy your statement at the same time you're issuing a holding statement or a press release. The last thing you want is for the members of your internal team to learn about the crisis on social media or hear Jake Tapper talk about it on CNN.

External Statements for Media and Social Platforms

When the heat is on, you can leverage your public-facing channels, including press releases, social media posts, and website pages, to frame the issues from your perspective. When creating your templates for various scenarios, lead with the human impact of the situation, explain your response, and demonstrate your values. Go live as soon as you can. External statements give you the chance to control the narrative before someone else does.

Regulatory Disclosure Templates

These are the compliance-ready messages that keep you out of legal trouble when your crisis has regulatory implications, financial issues, safety problems, or data breaches. Send these disclosures to regulators at the same time you go public or just before; never after. It's important to reach out to authorities and regulators before they reach out to you. I recommend vetting all statements through legal, but it's especially important to rely on your legal team when drafting regulatory disclosures.

Investor Communications for Material Events

Deploy this shareholder-focused messaging when a business disruption will move your stock price or affect earnings. Clearly address the financial impact, offer a recovery timeline, and exude leadership confidence. It's important to issue these communications before markets open or after they close to minimize volatility.

Step 4: Implement Monitoring and Early Warning Systems

Communications leaders need to develop a reflex reaction to any early warning signs that something could be amiss. The NFL's Katie Hill explains what having this type of trouble-spotting radar is like and why you need it.

As Katie points out, you can tell when a thing is going to become a thing. "As a communicator, it sounds unscientific and goofy, but it's so true. We all know people for whom everything is a crisis, every issue is DEFCON 1. But you have to be able to distinguish what matters, and that begins with monitoring," Katie explains. "You have to have world-class eyes across the landscape to get a sense of the canaries in the coal mine. In today's fragmenting media ecosystem, it's harder than ever to monitor in real time what's being said about you. But you have to do that."

This is why monitoring the public and internal relations landscapes is crucial to your crisis preparation protocols. The sooner you get wind of an issue, the better position you'll be in to address it or even contain it. Create an early warning arsenal that includes the following.

Internal Intelligence Networks

Often, your best early warning system can be the people closest to your stakeholders. Look to customer service, sales, your employees, and those engaged in government and investor relations for inside information on how your company is being perceived.

- **Customer service teams**: Talk to your customer service staff. Have they noticed any patterns with respect to complaints about your products, services, or personnel?

- **Sales teams**: Ask your sales force about customer reaction to your company. What are their customs really saying about your products or services? What is their overall perception of what's going on in your company or industry?
- **Employee feedback**: Collect intel through anonymous reporting systems and pulse surveys.
- **Government relations**: Talk to government relations people; they will have a pulse on any regulatory concerns or policy shifts that could spell trouble for your company.
- **Investor relations**: Your investor relations team can inform you of any shifts in market sentiment or ominous analyst chatter.

Digital Monitoring Tools

- **Media monitoring platforms**: Leverage the kind of actionable intelligence available through media monitoring platforms such as Meltwater, Cision, Alethea, and Talkwalker.
- **Social listening**: Track social media mentions for potential issues to gauge overarching sentiment as well as what kind of traction and velocity any conversations about your company are gaining across platforms.
- **Search trend monitoring**: Pay attention to Google Trends and any social platform trending topics that target or inform your company or industry.
- **Influencer tracking**: Who's talking about your company or industry, and how much reach do they have?

Key Performance Indicators

- **Conversation volume**: Determine your company's conversation levels to form a baseline across platforms and report on any spikes or significant declines.
- **Sentiment shifts**: Have people started discussing your company or brand differently? What does the shift look like? Positive? Negative? Neutral? Can you pinpoint trends over a particular time period? Keep in mind that a crisis that's handled well can actually move the needle in a positive direction.
- **Velocity metrics**: How fast are conversations spreading and multiplying? Are you dealing with a slow burn or a wildfire? The higher the velocity, the faster you need to move to outrun (and outmaneuver) the story.
- **Audience analysis**: Who's participating in the conversation about you—journalists, customers, employees, activists, or bots? Knowing who's driving the conversation will tell you how serious to take it.
- **Geographic tracking**: Where is attention concentrated? Is it local or intercontinental? Can you discern a pattern? Is it consistent or changing?

When it comes to keeping your ear to the ground, there's no such thing as being too vigilant. As Lisa Kaplan—whose company, Alethea, tracks disinformation campaigns—points out, ignoring the tea leaves can cost you: "If you ignore something posted on Telegram by an influencer who is known for driving narratives, you are being negligent, even though conventional wisdom tells you to ignore it until *The Wall Street Journal* calls. If there's a narrative gaining traction that could disrupt your business, you're running a real risk if you do nothing."

Step 5: Train Employees at All Levels

Crisis response training builds muscle memory; when the pressure hits, people revert to what they've practiced. You can't teach someone to swim when they're already drowning, which is why crisis prep training for both leadership and employees is so important. Teach your leadership team to act as your crisis cabinet and train your employees to be aware enough to function as your first line of defense.

Training Your Crisis Cabinet

Crisis Simulation Exercises

Often referred to as tabletop scenarios, these crisis simulation exercises test decision-making under pressure. I lead them with both executive teams and with the classes I teach at Northwestern. The goal is to get people to simulate the roles they would play in a crisis and see how well they execute those roles while the pressure is high, but the stakes are lower.

Executive Media Training

The purpose of media training is to make sure your leaders know how to think on their feet and respond authentically under pressure. You don't want your spokespeople to robotically reiterate talking points or come off like they're reading from a teleprompter.

Take the crisis scenarios you identified in your tabletop sessions and ask each participant to navigate the kind of worst-case scenario gotcha questions they might expect from a hostile press. Videotape the sessions so that you can critique every word and movement. Keep practicing until key messages come out naturally and body language supports this messaging.

Cross-Functional Collaboration

Think about how the different departments in your company can best work together in a crisis, and then bring those insights into your practice scenarios. Make sure everyone knows their role and shares their knowledge, insights, and ideas across functions.

Values-Based Decision-Making

Crises are often multifaceted, and you may find your team scrambling to balance competing pressures from different audiences. I was brought in to a company to train a leadership team on how to honor their commitment to diversity while walking a tightrope between the conflicting pressures they were receiving from employees, the public, and the administration. Leading with your values might sound simple, but that's not the case when you find yourself surrounded by stakeholders with competing interests. Work with your team to determine how you'll address these scenarios and how to incorporate values-based decision-making well before these issues rear their heads.

Employee Awareness: Your First Line of Defense

Most crises start small and then escalate. Your employees can be the first to see and report on the warning signs if they're given these tools and training to do so:

- **Recognition training**: Teach employees how to identify and report potential issues.
- **Escalation protocols**: Be clear on when they should report on a matter, who they should contact, and the best mechanism for reaching out given the circumstances.
- **Social media guidelines**: Every employee should be trained in your company's social media policies, including how to conduct themselves in a public forum during a company crisis

and how and when to sound the alarm if they notice harmful online activity.

- **Information security**: Develop and disseminate a protocol for protecting sensitive information, particularly in situations where discretion is required.

Practice Makes Permanent

If put on the shelf for too long, acquired skills become rusty. Training should be refreshed on an ongoing basis, preferably at a regular cadence:

- **Annual comprehensive simulations**: These full crisis team exercises are run by external facilitators and are designed to pop up unexpectedly to pressure-test the system. If possible, organize at least one of these a year, preferably when your team least expects it.
- **Quarterly scenario planning**: Once a quarter, gather your team for "what if" discussions around emerging risks.
- **Monthly team check-ins**: Schedule a time each month to practice your crisis communication and coordination protocols.
- **Real-time learning**: As soon as feasible following a crisis, bring your team together for post-incident debriefs, and integrate new lessons learned into your crisis plans.

Step 6: Review and Update Regularly: Staying Ahead of the Curve

Your crisis plan is a living document; it's not a museum piece. The threats you prepared for last year might not be the ones that hit you this year. If your company's Y2K holding statements are still taking up space in your template library, it's past time for a refresh.

I recommend conducting a strategic review of your crisis plan each year. Your assessment should cover:

- The evolving risk landscape to identify and assess any new threats that have emerged in your industry
- A team composition audit to determine if the right people are still in the right roles
- Verification of your contact database to see if the information you have on file is still current, as there's nothing worse than getting a "bounce back" in the middle of a crisis
- A technology and tools evaluation to determine if our monitoring systems are still best-in-class
- A look at regulatory and compliance updates to assess what's changed in your operating environment and whether there is potential new exposure to monitor

Some matters require a bit more vigilance. I recommend conducting quarterly tactical updates for:

- Scenario refinement to take into account changes in your industry and any emerging patterns that could cause concern
- Message testing to assess whether your holding statements still make sense and whether you need to add new ones to your template library
- Stakeholder mapping to determine if there have been changes to your key audiences or relevant influencers
- Resource assessment to determine whether your list of external resources, such as vendors and partners, is still reliable

AVOIDING THE STREISAND EFFECT: HOW TO TELL WHEN SILENCE IS GOLDEN

One of the most important strategic questions you'll face is this: When do you respond to a situation, and when do you let the fire burn out on its own?

This is a pain tolerance question that only you can answer.

Eleanor Hawkins, reporter at *Axios* and author of *Axios Communicators*, notes that the danger of triggering the Streisand effect, whereby attempting to suppress information actually makes it more widespread, needs to be addressed as a critical evolution in crisis management: "The Streisand effect has to be covered when talking about crisis evolution. Things are moving so quickly, very few messages penetrate mass audiences. What's the pain tolerance of a company before you need to respond? When am I giving it more oxygen, and when am I putting out the fire?"

Because the question of when to respond can be a difficult one, I offer the following response decision framework.

Always respond when:

- Safety issues are involved
- Core stakeholders (employees, customers, regulators) are asking questions
- False information could cause material business harm
- The story is gaining traction in places your key audiences actually pay attention to

Consider staying silent when:

- The criticism is coming from people who aren't your customers or key stakeholders
- Response would amplify a story that's already fading

- Engaging would drag you into a debate you can't win
- The story is trending but not among stakeholders who matter to your business

BUILDING EXTERNAL ALLIES AND SPOKESPERSON PREPARATION

Two critical elements of crisis preparation deserve their own detailed treatment: building relationships with external allies who can speak for you when you become your own worst messenger and identifying the right spokespeople for different crisis scenarios. We'll cover these comprehensively in later chapters, but here's what you need to know for baseline preparation.

External allies: The time to build relationships with academics, former officials, industry experts, and community leaders is before you need them to give you the benefit of the doubt. Start now; we'll cover the strategy in detail later.

Spokesperson selection: The right spokesperson is whoever can deliver your message most credibly to your most important audience, not necessarily the person with the biggest title. Build a bench of trained spokespeople across different expertise areas and crisis types. More on this in chapter 10.

DON'T GET CAUGHT SLIPPIN'

Crisis preparation *isn't* paranoia; it's survival. And survival requires more than good intentions and smart people. It requires systems, relationships, and practice.

Key Learnings:

- Invest in crisis preparation, not just responses.
- Small teams make big decisions. Create a war cabinet of five to seven people rather than a committee that drags down decision-making.
- Simple systems beat complex procedures, which is why you need to adopt frameworks that work at 2:00 a.m. under pressure. Speed requires structure.
- Build your relationships; they're your crisis currency.

PART TWO

THE PATH FORWARD

NEW AGE OF CRISIS RESPONSE

CHAPTER NINE

STOP TALKING TO EMPTY ROOMS

Imagine that the CEO of a top solar energy company is facing a crisis over manufacturing delays threatening a major utility contract. The communications team springs into action, securing perfect placement in *The Wall Street Journal* and a follow-up on CNBC's *Power Lunch*. The CEO delivers flawlessly, acknowledging challenges, outlining recovery, and reinforcing clean energy commitment.

The problem? The people most impacted by this crisis weren't reading the *Journal*. The utility executives making the contract decision, the project managers on the ground, and the renewable energy procurement specialists are getting their updates from *Solar Power World*'s daily newsletter. They're following and discussing developments through the Clean Energy LinkedIn community and listening to the *Energy Gang* podcast during commutes. Local news stations are covering the delays, community boards are lighting up with concerns about rising energy costs, and Facebook groups are exploding with frustrated residents discussing how these investments were supposed to help ease utility bills.

And none of these forums are carrying the CEO's message.

Instead of meeting his audience where they were, the CEO was speaking to general business readers while his actual stakeholders were consuming information through channels his team had never considered.

Perfect message.

Flawless execution.

Wrong audience.

Leaders often find themselves shouting into the wind, not because their message is wrong but because they're addressing an empty arena.

Seasoned communicators understand the benefits of precision targeting. Here's how Michael Marinello, global head of communications for JPMorgan Payments, navigates today's fragmented media landscape: "First, identify the most impacted or important audience that needs to hear your message, given the situation. Second, determine the best and most appropriate channels for delivering your information to them. Third, be direct and succinct in your language, leaving no room for ambiguity. Fourth, monitor the outputs and measure the impact so you can adjust and adapt if necessary."

And it all begins with understanding the intersections of influence, strategy, and business impact.

WHO ACTUALLY HAS POWER OVER YOUR BUSINESS?

If you're like many of my early clients, you've got great monitoring tools, solid reputation research, and an experienced team that executes well 90 percent of the time. But when a crisis hits, you're flying blind when making the decisions that matter most.

Your CEO wants to see *The Wall Street Journal* coverage, while your chief financial officer (CFO) wants proof that communications spending drives actual business outcomes. Your team delivers. But deep down, you know you're not being as strategic as you could be about where to focus your energy and resources.

One of my goals is to help my clients to stop thinking about investors or policymakers as monolithic audiences. Instead, I encourage them to start thinking about influence as a strategy to be applied in concentric circles based on business impact. In my own experiences, this shift makes all the difference.

THE SCHUMER TEST: POTENTIAL IMPACT DOESN'T EQUAL ACTUAL IMPACT

January 29, 2018. I'm at my desk at UTC, which at the time owned Carrier, when alerts start flying. Senate Minority Leader Chuck Schumer just called out our company by name on the Senate floor. "Carrier, a company the president promised to save, continues to bleed jobs," he said. "They are a metaphor. A lot of nice announcements, a lot of bits of glitz, but actually, the condition of the American worker is not getting much better."[65]

My phone exploded. Leadership went into full panic mode. One of the most powerful lawmakers in the country had just tied us to Trump's failed promises on national TV.

But our real-time stakeholder-monitoring system was telling a different story. Yes, there was a conversation spike immediately after

65 "Schumer Floor Remarks on Urgency to Work on Legislative Priorities Before February 8th and the Republican Tax Bill," US Senate Democratic Caucus, January 24, 2018, https://www.democrats.senate.gov/newsroom/press-releases/schumer-floor-remarks-on-urgency-to-work-on-legislative-priorities-before-february-8th-and-the-republican-tax-bill.

Schumer's remarks. Social media lit up. A few reporters mentioned it. But then something interesting happened: Within thirty minutes, the conversation started dropping off. No pickup among defense appropriators. No engagement from the regulators who scrutinized our operations. No discussion among the industry analysts who influenced our investors.

Here's the crucial detail that made this a teaching moment rather than a crisis: Schumer absolutely had the power to hurt us. As Senate minority leader, he could have called committee hearings, pushed for investigations, and rallied other senators to take action. But in this particular moment, through the vehicle he chose—a floor speech not tied to any vote or legislative action—his impact was symbolic, not substantive.

Not every word spoken by a powerful person has a powerful impact. Context matters.

Our data showed exactly what was happening: outer circle (e.g., general public) noise with no inner circle (e.g., real opinion driver) momentum.

So, I told leadership, "The best thing we can do right now is nothing."

If we issued a statement, we'd amplify a narrative that was already dying on its own. We'd risk extending a story that the next news cycle would naturally knock out if we let it.

I gained valuable insight that day. Not every word spoken by a powerful person has a powerful impact. Context matters. Your job is to measure *actual* impact among your priority audiences, not react to hypothetical influence.

In the current environment, you're going to get hit. What determines your survival isn't whether you get hit; it's whether the people who impact your business outcomes will defend you when you need it most. And that requires knowing exactly who those people are, what they care about, and where they get the information that drives their decisions about your company.

IDENTIFYING YOUR PRIORITY AUDIENCES

A lot of people are going to have opinions about your business during a crisis, and some of those opinions can cause your business harm. You'll never be able to manage every conversation around a crisis or mold every opinion to your way of thinking. The companies most likely to survive a crisis know better than to even try. The companies that make it through are the ones that have taken the time to learn who can help or harm them during a crisis and have taken the necessary steps to foster and protect relationships with these influencers well before a crisis puts them to the test.

And that starts with defining your inner, middle, and outer circles of influence.

Your Inner Circle: Direct Business Impact

Your inner circle consists of the people who can immediately affect your operations. Usually, this will consist of just a handful of impactful stakeholders. When identifying your inner circle, consider the following:

- The top few regulators who control your key licenses
- Leadership and procurement teams at your top-tier customers
- Portfolio managers at your major institutional investors
- Your critical suppliers who could disrupt operations
- Government officials who write and enforce the rules affecting your sector

Middle Circle: Influence Amplifiers

Your middle circle of influencers has the power to shape what your inner circle thinks. Typically, it will consist of between fifteen and fifty stakeholders, which will include:

- The handful of industry reporters and content creators your stakeholders actually listen to
- Trade association leaders who brief your regulators
- Your senior employees who validate claims to customers
- The analysts your investors consult for sector guidance
- Community leaders in markets where you operate facilities

Outer Circle: General Awareness (Everyone Else)

The outer circle consists largely of people who are great at creating noise but generally have little significant influence, as they rarely drive business decisions. These include the following:

- Fringe media personalities
- Most social media influencers
- Members of the general public (outside of your target demographic)
- Activist groups seeking attention
- Politicians not directly relevant to your business making statements

You can't completely ignore this group; even people who are not traditional stakeholders of your business can do you harm if motivated. The key is not to over-index on them.

Once you've determined who fits into which circle, it's time to use this knowledge to make decisions regarding resource allocation.

I recommend focusing 70 percent of your crisis preparation and response on the inner circle, 25 percent on the middle circle, and just 5 percent on maintaining awareness of the outer circle. You only have so much time and resources. So, put your energy into the people who can significantly impact perceptions where they count the most.

MAPPING YOUR REAL DECISION-MAKERS

As you're compiling your list of real influencers and decision-makers and determining which circle they belong in, be as detailed as possible. Take your current stakeholder list and be brutally specific. Replace "customers" with "Sarah Johnson in supply chain procurement at Global Corp, who controls our $50 million contract renewal." Replace "regulators" with "Mike Chen at EPA Region 5, who approves our key facility permits."

Then, apply this business impact test. For each stakeholder, ask, "If this person changed their opinion about us tomorrow, what specific business outcome would change within ninety days?"

If you can't answer that question concretely, they belong in a lower circle.

KNOW WHERE YOUR AUDIENCES ACTUALLY CONSUME INFORMATION

Identifying your stakeholders and decision-makers in order of influence is one thing, but understanding how and where to reach them is another. This is where it's vitally important to understand the new media landscape and how to leverage it to your advantage in a way that ensures your messaging gets to its intended audience.

The New Media Landscape Reality Check

Audiences have atomized. The old playbook of securing placement in prestige outlets no longer guarantees you'll reach the people who actually matter to your business. Success now requires surgical precision in determining where your stakeholders consume information and the courage to meet them there, even when it feels uncomfortable. Creating content for the greatest impact—including how, why, and when to leverage prestige outlets to reach your goals—is covered in detail in chapter 11.

And a quick note: Cultural lobbying, a concept pioneered by my BPI partner Greg Propper, recognizes that elite opinion drivers consume culture—including sports, TV, and social media—just like everyone else, making cultural channels often more effective than traditional media or lobbying for introducing important topics. So, instead of pitching media, sometimes the strongest pitch is to an artist, a creator, or a TV writers' room, because culture sits above politics and can cut through polarized groups and topics. The key is understanding that culture isn't a side door to policy change; it's the front door through which people form their beliefs and identities.

STRATEGIC AUDIENCE MAPPING: THE FOUR-QUESTION METHOD

Stop asking "Where can we get coverage?" and start asking "Where are the people we need to reach actually paying attention?" Break it down by knowing the answers to the following four questions, then use the answers to target your communications based on your desired outcomes.

Question 1: Who specifically needs to hear this message?
The answer here should never be simply "business leaders." You need to be definitive about which business leaders. Does your message need to reach CFOs concerned about regulatory compliance? Board members evaluating environmental, social, and governance (ESG) risk? IT executives looking to upgrade their antiquated data storage systems?

The specificity here is needed to determine everything else.

Question 2: Where do they consume information?
The answer here is not where you think they *should* be consuming information but rather where they actually go for information. Your target CFOs might get more financial news from Fintwit than from the *Financial Times*.

Question 3: What is the preferred format for each space?
Craft your messaging to fit the platform and its intended audience. For instance, position executive summaries on LinkedIn. Schedule your CEO for interviews on deep-dive podcasts that air during commutes. Focus on providing more compelling imagery on Instagram. Different platforms reward different content types.

Question 4: What would make them take action?
Awareness isn't enough; you need to think about what drives behavior change. Is it peer validation? Data that contradicts their assumptions? A clear call to action with specific next steps? Messaging should always be created with action in mind.

Target Stages Based on Desired Outcomes

You'll want to stage your message with the desired outcome in mind, whether you're building awareness among stakeholders, guiding them as they explore the issue and consider their options, or preparing them to make decisions that impact your business.

- **Awareness stage**: Focus on broad-reach platforms and viral potential. Social media, streaming advertising, and influencer partnerships work best when you need maximum eyeballs on a message quickly.
- **Consideration stage**: Deploy trusted voices and detailed content. Industry newsletters, expert podcasts, and peer testimonials matter most when stakeholders are actively evaluating options.
- **Decision stage**: Leverage peer validation and authoritative sources. Board-level conversations happen through different channels than consumer awareness campaigns. Think private briefings, industry events, and direct executive engagement.

BUILDING YOUR STAKEHOLDER INTELLIGENCE SYSTEM

Before the incident with Senator Schumer calling out Carrier, UTC's government relations chief, Tim McBride, had challenged my team and me to build a real-time stakeholder intelligence system that connected directly to business outcomes. Because we had that system in place, I was able to advise the executive team that the best course of action was no action. Having a stakeholder intelligence system proved beneficial on several levels and in several situations; it actually allowed us to head off multiple potential crises, redirect resources from noncrisis situations, and provide concrete impact data on communications investments we chose to make.

Stakeholder Intelligence System Components

If your company is like most, you're likely tracking mentions and sentiment across broad audiences. That's great for making reports but not for driving decisions. What you need is intelligence about specific decision-makers so you can make better strategic choices.

A stakeholder intelligence system provides intelligence that can drive decisions.

Creating Your Own Stakeholder Intelligence System

Creating a bespoke shareholder intelligence system begins with stakeholder intelligence gathering:

- **Information diet analysis**: First, determine where your inner-circle stakeholders actually get information. (Hint: It's probably not where you think.)
- **Influence network mapping**: Next, determine who your inner circle's influencers are. Who do they talk to when forming their opinions about companies such as yours?
- **Decision-making timeline tracking**: When do your inner-circle stakeholders make the choices that affect your business?
- **Trust and credibility auditing**: Which sources and spokespeople do they find most credible?

Tracking all of this might sound time-consuming or even cost-prohibitive. It doesn't have to be. Instead of monitoring everything, monitor the ten information sources your top twenty stakeholders actually consume. If you are close to the individual, ask them what they read and note which publications they reference. If not, ask those in your orbit who might be closer. If your target is a public figure, note where they are most often quoted and written about. You'll get better intelligence while spending less.

Now that you've gathered the intelligence you need, you'll be able to make informed and sound decisions on whether, where, and how to proceed with getting your messaging out to your most important audience. When it comes to where, don't make the mistake of just seeking out friendly vehicles. Sometimes, the best strategy includes wading into hostile territory.

EMBRACE (AND EARN) THE CREDIBILITY DIVIDEND

Leaders who only appear in friendly territory get dismissed as echo chamber participants. Those willing to engage tough but fair audiences earn a credibility dividend that carries over to all their communications.

Donald Trump's appearance at the National Association of Black Journalists (NABJ) convention as a second-time presidential candidate in 2024 sparked intense internal debate and drew record attendance—over 3,625 registered attendees, making it the second-highest attended NABJ convention ever. His interview with ABC's Rachel Scott quickly turned contentious when she opened with tough questions about his past statements on race. Despite the hostile reception, the appearance generated massive coverage across all media platforms and demonstrated the power of showing up where you're not automatically welcomed.

Former Biden administration Secretary of Transportation Pete Buttigieg's Fox News appearances consistently go viral, with his measured tone and fact-based rebuttals earning praise even from political opponents. As he told PBS News, "I can't blame somebody for not supporting my perspective if they've literally never heard it."[66]

Congressman Ro Khanna frequently appears on conservative platforms, and that's by design. Marie Baldassarre, chief of staff for Congressman Khanna, put it this way: "You reach people you otherwise wouldn't—so why not show up?" She believes showing up, especially in spaces where disagreement is likely, is an opportunity, not a liability:

"One of the things Ro used to get hit on more is this idea that when you go on right-wing platforms, you're giving them legitimacy. And our argument has always been that they already have the viewers and the audience, and it's really your moment to speak directly to these people that you would otherwise not reach … You don't back away from your values. You prepare for the hot-button topics, and you go in with clear, concise arguments—and also look for common ground where you can."

Preparation Strategy

To Marie's point, you need to prepare before you enter hostile territory. You can't expect the interviewer to pull any punches, so you have to be prepared for worst-case questions. In fact, expect them to ask the thing you hope they won't, and know exactly how you'll respond. Know your three strongest points cold. To stand up against hostile fire, you need to have your core messages so internalized that aggressive interruptions can't knock you off track. You'll need specific examples at the ready; concrete stories and data points are harder to dismiss than abstract policy positions or pre-rehearsed talking points.

---

66 Pete Buttigieg, "Mayor Pete Buttigieg Addresses Controversial Comments," interview by the panel, The View, November 3, 2020, https://www.youtube.com/watch?v=dF7DyUf6grE.

WHAT ACTUALLY PROTECTS YOU (AND WHAT DOESN'T)

My BPI colleagues, Danny Franklin and Matt Carter have led groundbreaking, evidence-based work in separate instances to reveal why some companies survive crises while others don't. The findings suggest it's not what most communications teams prioritize.

The breakthrough finding: There's a massive difference between stakeholders who like your company and those who will defend it when things go bad. Companies with identical trust levels can have completely different crisis vulnerabilities. More than half (53 percent) of consumers believe any given piece of misinformation about the average company. But some companies are 1.7 times more vulnerable than others with similar trust profiles.[67]

So what actually creates stakeholder resilience? What turns a stakeholder into a staunch defender, especially in times of trouble? As my partner, Danny Franklin, shared with PRovoke Media,

> The most powerful predictors get back to some direct relationship that people have with a brand.
>
> The ones that we saw being really powerful are first having leadership that cares about something other than just profit, being a company that is led by values, a real sense of your purpose as a company.

Also important were attributes related to product quality and willingness to improve products constantly; to employee well-being, such

67 Paul Holmes, "Bully Pulpit Study: What Makes Brands Resilient in Crisis," PRovoke Media, April 8, 2025, https://www.provokemedia.com/latest/article/bully-pulpit-study-what-makes-brands-resilient-in-crisis.

as offering good pay and benefits; and "the impact that you're having on communities, creating jobs that strengthen the community."[68]

If your company is like many that I've worked with, you're probably investing too much in broad awareness building at the expense of shoring up your relationship with your inner circle. Some of the areas that companies overinvest in include the following:

- General brand awareness campaigns
- Broad-reach media coverage
- Executive thought leadership in general business publications

Think about reallocating resources to solidifying key stakeholder relationships. The return on investment (ROI) of key stakeholder relationship building versus general media relations isn't even close.

THE DATA-DRIVEN APPROACH TO AUDIENCE ENGAGEMENT

American consumers now spend around eight hours daily on digital media, roughly double the time invested in traditional formats. Digital video viewing time overtook traditional TV in 2024, with US adults spending two hours and fifty-three minutes daily on digital video versus two hours and forty-eight minutes on traditional TV.

Connected TV and Streaming

As of 2022, less than 50 percent of US households subscribe to pay TV, with cord-cutting accelerating faster than expected. However, they're still watching video content, just not how traditional advertis-

68 Holmes, "Bully Pulpit Study."

ers expect. Connected TV advertising now allows precision targeting that broadcast never could.[69]

Streaming viewers actively choose what to watch rather than passively consuming whatever is on. This creates higher engagement rates but requires content that earns attention rather than simply interrupting it. When considering where to place your communications efforts, focus on the metrics that matter:

- **Engagement over impressions**: One thousand engaged stakeholders beats one hundred thousand passive views.
- **Action over awareness**: Track behavior change, not just message recall.
- **Influence mapping**: Who do your stakeholders trust? Start there.

Be prepared to revise your metrics and adapt your analyses as new technologies emerge and tastes evolve. Where audiences gather shifts constantly. What worked six months ago may be irrelevant today. Build systems to track audience migration, not just campaign performance.

PRACTICAL Q&A THAT DRIVES BETTER DECISIONS

Before any major communications initiative, be sure that you've assembled a team of experts who can help develop an actionable communications plan that reaches your specific goal.

Start with these questions:

---

69 "Less than 50% of US Households Now Subscribe to Pay TV, as Cord-Cutting Jumps More than Expected," eMarketer, March 7, 2023, https://www.emarketer.com/press-releases/less-than-50-of-us-households-now-subscribe-to-pay-tv-as-cord-cutting-jumps-more-than-expected.

1. Who are the twenty people whose opinion change could affect our business within ninety days?
2. Where do these specific people get the information they use for professional decisions?
3. What would actually change their behavior toward us? (Be specific about actions, not attitudes.)
4. How will we measure whether we've influenced the people who matter?
5. What's the opportunity cost of broad reach versus targeted stakeholder engagement?

THE ROI CONVERSATION YOU CAN FINALLY HAVE

Most comms leaders struggle to articulate a clear connection between communications costs and business outcomes. The following framework can help facilitate a meaningful ROI conversation with your CEO and CFO and get their buy-in for moving forward with a focused and, ultimately, more efficient and cost-effective communications strategy.

Explain to your CEO that instead of trying to influence everyone, you're focusing 70 percent of your resources on the twenty stakeholders who control 80 percent of your business risk. Then, provide your methodology for measuring success with this population, as well as the business impact and efficacy of this laser focus.

When explaining this strategy to your CFO, detail how putting resources into communications with this clear focus will prevent even more costly—and potentially devastating—outcomes. For example, you could explain, "In the past six months, our targeted stakeholder engagement approach prevented regulatory action that would have cost $X, preserved customer relationships worth $Y, and maintained investor confidence that supports our stock price."

Include your team in the buy-in process by letting them know that you're moving forward with a strategic approach that focuses on clear priorities based on business impact rather than traditional media metrics. They'll need to shift their thinking a bit, but the impact of their efforts in gaining the results you're after will speak for itself.

ON STAKEHOLDER MISALIGNMENT AND BUILDING COMMUNITIES

Just as building systems to align your actions and messages with your core stakeholders can significantly advance your business, the inverse is also true. Failing to meet your stakeholders where they're at can have devastating consequences. Eleanor Hawkins from *Axios* used the example of Tesla to illustrate how even successful companies can face severe backlash when leadership actions contradict core customer values. As she points out, Elon Musk's political engagement fundamentally conflicted with Tesla's environmentally conscious consumer base.

"Elon Musk and Tesla's takedown is mainly because his consumer base was not aligned with the actions he was taking as head of DOGE. It's not just identifying your stakeholders, but knowing them—knowing how they feel, knowing where they stand."

The attention economy has fundamentally changed stakeholder engagement. Companies must now think like political campaigns in building devoted communities.

"It's no longer just that you have to find a community; you now have to build a cult, basically," Eleanor says. "You really do have to generate more than just a passive audience. Which cult do I need to create? Engineers? Investors? Gen Z consumers? All of these are strategies that have been used in politics for decades."

Key Learnings:

In crisis communications, everyone has an opinion, but only a few people's opinions can actually hurt your business. Your job isn't to try to manage every conversation; it's to identify the conversations that matter and engage to protect those relationships before a crisis tests them.

The companies that survive aren't those with the most positive media coverage. They're the ones whose critical stakeholders will give them the benefit of the doubt when it matters most.

Successful crisis communicators can make a strategic shift from broad reputation management to targeted stakeholder relationship building. From measuring impressions to measuring influence. From reactive crisis response to proactive resilience building. And they can do this by:

- Making data-informed, outcomes-oriented decisions about where to engage
- Understanding that what matters more than where they say something is who hears it and that where they need to focus their messaging is constantly changing
- Being willing to engage tough audiences so they build credibility everywhere; strategic discomfort beats comfortable irrelevance

Your message is only as good as your ability to put it in front of the right people. In today's fragmented media landscape, this requires abandoning prestige for precision and comfort for impact.

CHAPTER TEN

MASTER THE MESSAGE

SOUND BITES, SUBSTANCE, AND STRATEGIC VOICES

Every crisis is a real-life drama, demanding a problem, a victim, a villain, a hero, and a resolution. Your goal as a crisis communicator is to keep your organization from being cast as the villain. And you accomplish that goal by telling a compelling story with a strong narrative from your point of view.

Organizations that simply present facts without assigning narrative roles lose control of the story, risking getting cast as the villain by default. The solution isn't just to be mindful of what you say but to be strategic when it comes to how you state your message, who acts as spokesperson, and where your message appears.

I'm not just positing a theory here. I've seen executives get humiliated because they refused to understand the importance of controlling how their story was being told and who would fulfill which roles in the narrative drama. I've watched companies hemorrhage value because they thought the facts just automatically and naturally spoke for themselves. I've also seen organizations seize control of devastating situations by deliberately casting roles and strategically choosing their characters' voices.

Mastering the art of the narrative is crucial, and it begins with understanding the dramatic arc of crisis communications, starting with the importance of story structure in a crisis.

WHY STORY STRUCTURE MATTERS IN A CRISIS

If your crisis communications revolve around data points alone, you're missing a critical opportunity to connect with your audience. Even worse, you're abdicating control of the narrative to whoever chooses to drive it.

The human brain doesn't process crises as data points; it processes crises as stories. And every story needs characters with clear roles. Organizations that fail to cast the people who will fill these dramatic roles end up leaving the audience no choice but to assign the roles themselves. And nine times out of ten, when left to their own devices, the public will cast a company and its executives as the villains.

Take the executive who found himself in front of an investigativereporter after a major technical failure led to customers being hurt. The reporter demanded to know who had been fired for the mistake. The leader's instinct was to protect his team and refuse to create scapegoats. He said that, as a policy, he doesn't comment on personnel matters. Noble? Absolutely. Smart? Not entirely.

His refusal to confirm that anyone had been fired (several people had been) was not perceived as leadership; it was perceived as a lack of accountability. By trying to be the hero who protects his people, he unwittingly cast the company as the villain hiding behind lawyers and PR spin. The narrative wrote itself: *executive dodges basic questions, refuses to say who's accountable.*

He lost control of the story the moment he misunderstood his role in it, which should have been to acknowledge the severity of the situation and make clear that the company had taken, and would continue to take, all necessary actions to ensure that something like that mistake would never happen again. I told the executive to run it by legal, but if he could at least say that *X* employees were terminated within *Y* days of the completion of the company's investigation, the organization may not be viewed as a hero, but it could create the perception that the company was working to punish the villains. After some work to clarify the record in a follow-up interview, the new narrative helped shift the conversation.

Compare that to how Turo managed the narrative during the 2025 New Year's terror attacks in New Orleans and Las Vegas. As you might recall, terrorists in both cities rented trucks through Turo to carry out heinous attacks, putting the rideshare platform squarely in the crosshairs of a story about terrorism and public safety. Instead of retreating, Turo immediately positioned itself as a concerned corporate citizen, empathizing with victims, working with authorities, and immediately taking affirmative steps to prevent future tragedies. Through these efforts, it successfully nixed a narrative that could have called it out as a spineless platform that enabled violence.

I was interviewed for a piece in *PR Daily* a few days after the attacks and offered this observation on Turo's response:

> [*Turo*] *showed not only remorse, but care for those who were impacted, but then quickly moved from there into really dictating all of the ways that one, they're working to make the app safe, and have traditionally worked to make the app safe, but two, that they were going to be working hand-in-hand*

> *with authorities to ensure they could get to the bottom of what happened in these instances and apply that to anything they may need to change about their own approach moving forward.*[70]

Turo didn't just respond to the story. It helped write it through bold statements that imparted empathy, accountability, and cooperation.

Tactical Takeaway: Map Your Roles

Before you say a word in public, ask yourself these questions: Who are we in this story? Are we the victim of circumstance? The hero working toward a resolution? Or are we accidentally positioning ourselves as the antagonist that is creating obstacles to answers?

I'm not saying there's never value in playing the villain, just that you should never let yourself become the villain by default. Sure, most of the time, you'll want to cast yourself as a hero or a victim, but there may be times you'll actually decide it's in your best interest to cast yourself as the villain, as counterintuitive as that may seem. Sometimes, leaning into the villain role serves your strategic objectives better than fighting it. You might adopt the strategy that if you're going to be cast as the heavy anyway, it's in your best interest to own it completely. President Trump has used this tactic very effectively to gain leverage in trade negotiations, most visibly through his tariff strategy. My point is that you—and you alone—need to fulfill the role of central casting here so that you drive the narrative in the direction that you need it to go. If you do end up the villain, make sure it's because *you* made the calculated decision to adopt that role.

---

70 Allison Carter, "Crisis Lessons from Turo's Response to New Year's Day Attacks," *PR Daily*, January 13, 2025, https://www.prdaily.com/crisis-lessons-from-turos-response-to-new-years-day-attacks/.

The framework is simple: Map every stakeholder to a role, understand which role you're naturally falling into, and then decide if that serves your objectives. If it doesn't, reframe your role thoughtfully and deliberately.

THE SOUND-BITE REALITY: 4.2 SECONDS TO WIN OR LOSE

We are all operating in a shrinking attention economy. In 1968, during Nixon's presidential run, the average TV sound bite lasted 42.3 seconds.[71] Today, you get nine seconds. That's not a typo; nine seconds reflects the brutal math of modern attention spans.

This shrinking window creates a paradoxical environment that most communications professionals fail to confront: You need to be substantive yet pithy, comprehensive yet concise, memorable yet accurate. All at the same time. All in barely more time than it takes to sneeze.

Donald Trump has mastered this reality better than any leader I've studied. His sound bites aren't accidents; they're engineered. Take any complex issue, define a clear point of view, isolate the key takeaway, find a visual analogy, and craft the tightest possible delivery. Alliteration and rhythm work. Repetition works. Making people feel something works.

CEOs who dismiss this tactic as beneath them are making a fatal mistake. Your nuanced, thoughtful, technically accurate response will

71 Kiku Adatto, "Sound Bite Democracy: Network Evening News Presidential Campaign Coverage, 1968 and 1988," Shorenstein Center on Media, Politics and Public Policy, Harvard University, June 1990, https://shorensteincenter.org/wp-content/uploads/2012/03/r02_adatto.pdf; Stephen Farnsworth and S. Robert Lichter, *The Nightly News Nightmare*, 3rd ed. (Routledge, 2011).

get buried under your competitor's memorable three-word phrase every time.

The Sound-Bite Formula

The process of converting what you want to convey into strategic sound bites requires discipline and a few key steps:

1. Take the complex issue and strip it to its essential conflict.
2. Define your clear point of view on that conflict.
3. Isolate the key takeaway that you need your audience to remember.
4. Find a visual analogy that helps make an abstract concept concrete.
5. Craft the tightest possible delivery using rhythm and repetition.

The Avoiding Quotability Tactic

There's a flip side to coming up with a quotable sound bite, and that's creating a scenario in which you appear accessible while providing no sound bite at all. It's useful to deploy this tactic when it's in your best interest to contribute to a narrative without necessarily jumping into the fray.

I once worked with a CFO who consistently spoke with reporters to shape their understanding of complex financial challenges. One reporter who was one of the most frequent requestors of these briefings bemoaned to me after one of them that the CFO "says so much, but never anything specific enough to make news." That wasn't a bug; it was a feature.

The CFO was making a tactical play. While other executives were getting burned by out-of-context quotes, he was building relationships and credibility without opening himself and his company up to liability. Sometimes, talking without really talking is exactly what the moment requires.

Language Land Mines

Every crisis communications plan should include a "never say this" list, because certain phrases will detonate regardless of your intent.

I learned this lesson the hard way during a Boeing layoff situation. I described how Boeing was able to "take advantage of" a learning opportunity during the restructuring process, and when the story was published, the quote made it sound like we exploited employees. The phrase *take advantage* carries a completely different weight in the context of human cost versus competitive advantage.

You can *take advantage* in sports, business deals, or market opportunities. You should not *take advantage* when people are losing their jobs, getting sick, or facing real harm. The context transforms the meaning, and intent becomes irrelevant.

Build your land mine list now, before a crisis hits. Include obvious ones, such as "acceptable losses" or "collateral damage," but also test your standard corporate language against human scenarios. Does "optimize our workforce" sound different when people are losing their homes after being laid off? It should.

MATCHING URGENCY OF MESSAGE TO MEDIUM

Not every crisis plays by the same rules. The communication strategy that works for a data breach will destroy you during a safety recall. The type of crisis determines everything about how you deploy your message.

Safety Crises: Credibility First, Speed Second

When people's physical safety is at stake, such as in the case of toxic spills, product recalls, or active threats, credibility is your only currency. Lead with your most credible channels: direct website alerts, straight-to-camera CEO video, and immediate SMS and email notifications where possible.

Let traditional media amplify your official message rather than hoping viral spread gets there first. In safety crises, you want shares of credible reporting, not shares of speculation. Print press and local broadcast in the most impacted areas carry more weight than a thousand retweets.

The goal isn't virality; it's trust. And trust travels through different networks than entertainment.

Reputational Crises: Mind-Changing, Not Lifesaving

Reputational crises play by different rules because you're changing minds, not protecting lives. This requires broader stakeholder engagement and content tailored to break through on each platform.

Consider how the B2B SaaS company Astronomer handled the viral video of its CEO and HR head being caught embracing on the Jumbotron during a "kiss cam" moment at a July 2025 Coldplay concert in Foxboro, Massachusetts. Even though the company had a very discreet circle of stakeholders, public fascination with the incident threatened to consume all available airtime with their actual customers. The public was having a field day parodying the infamous hug and duck at sporting events and concerts for weeks. And don't get me started on the memes. As my sister says, our adulterous friends broke the internet.

Astronomer's solution? It hired Gwyneth Paltrow as a temporary spokesperson and placed a viral digital ad to satisfy cultural curiosity.

The Paltrow video wasn't meant to address Astronomer's actual customers; it was meant to move public attention along so the company could do the serious work of repairing its reputation with its core stakeholders without intense scrutiny.

Different games, different rules, different measures of success.

SPOKESPERSON STRATEGY: VOICE, VENUE, AND TIMING

The days of one-size-fits-all spokespeople are over. Your CEO's LinkedIn presence needs different content than your Instagram strategy, which needs different voices than your podcast appearances.

	CEO	LOCAL LEADER	SUBJECT EXPERT	MEDIA RELATIONS	LEGAL COUNSEL	INVESTOR RELATIONS	EXTERNAL (POLICE, REGULATOR)
ENTERPRISE-LEVEL BUSINESS FAILURE	×			×		×	
SITE-SPECIFIC SAFETY ISSUE		×		×			×
MAJOR LAWSUIT				×	×		
LARGE SCALE PRODUCT ISSUE	×		×	×		×	×
WORKFORCE ISSUE/ REDUCTION	×	×	×	×		×	

The right spokesperson is whoever can deliver the message *most credibly* to an audience.

Match voice to venue and avoid forcing square pegs into round holes. Your CFO's thoughtful analysis of market conditions might be perfect for a *Bloomberg* interview but terrible for a TikTok response to criticism. The CEO's quotes work for traditional media and LinkedIn. But do you have younger employees who can break down that same message for Instagram and TikTok in digestible formats? Can you create shareable infographics for X and Facebook? Is there a credible, articulate technical executive who makes more sense for long-form podcast breakdowns?

Keep in mind that the right spokesperson isn't always the one with the biggest title. Think about who can deliver your message most credibly to your specific audience at that specific moment. This creates a strategic matrix most companies don't think through: Spokesperson selection depends on topic, audience, *and* sequence of updates. Your CEO might need to make the opening statement, but a subject matter expert might need to handle all technical follow-ups. Your head of HR might be the right voice for internal communications, while your legal counsel handles regulatory conversations.

Credibility trumps hierarchy. Every time.

The Rev. Jackson Lesson: Authority Commands Calm

I learned the most important lesson about spokesperson authority during a fifteen-thousand-person Chicago rally for DREAM Act kids in 2010. I stood on stage behind Rev. Jackson as he delivered a barn burner of a speech. After he finished, one of the organizers pulled out a bullhorn and started shouting vitriol at and about Rev. Jackson, falsely claiming that he was attempting to make the event about himself by "stealing the headlines." Suddenly, we found ourselves in a swarm of thousands of people, some angry, many confused. This situation was volatile and becoming increasingly dangerous for us all. In the center of this crowd, Rev. Jackson's security looked at me and said, "I'm only here to protect one person," and it wasn't me.

To diffuse the situation, Rev. Jackson simply lifted his hand and said, "Everybody, calm down. We're all on the same team here. Let's all go back."

The crowd immediately complied.

A million people could have said those exact words. But Rev. Jackson's grounding, his earned authority, and his track record of being exactly where he said he'd be commanded instant trust. In a crisis, having someone who can reestablish trust with that kind of automatic credibility is extraordinarily powerful.

You can't manufacture that authority in the middle of a crisis. You build it over years.

Case Studies in Strategic Voice

During the intense scrutiny surrounding Microsoft's acquisition of Activision Blizzard in 2023, then-Activision CCO Lulu Cheng Meservey responded to detractors directly, bypassing traditional media entirely as she masterfully translated legal filings into plain English. Her approach worked because she had genuine expertise and wasn't afraid to engage in hand-to-hand combat with critics on their own platforms.

But this isn't exactly a new playbook. A decade earlier, David Tovar, vice president of communications at Walmart at the time, delivered one of the most successful early examples of this approach. When *The New York Times* published an op-ed critical of Walmart's labor practices, Tovar didn't just send a letter to the editor or wait for a correction.

Rather than a standard response, Tovar edited the piece line by line in red pen like a high school English teacher and posted the markup on Walmart's official blog. It was bold, funny, and most importantly, effective. The post went viral, completely reframing the conversation. Walmart didn't need to ask for a correction; it became the corrector. Like Lulu's strategy, it worked because it was direct and timely and carried a distinct voice.

And it doesn't always need to be combative. Alan Epstein at Pratt & Whitney was a Massachusetts Institute of Technology PhD who served as vice president of Science & Technology, leading a small team. His primary responsibilities included research and advocating on behalf of the company. He dedicated significant time to defending and advancing company positions across media, government committees, Congress, and scientific journals. He was successful as a company spokesperson because he was the real deal: a bona fide research engineer who could speak with unquestionable authority.

The pattern isn't complicated: Genuine expertise plus communication skill plus willingness to engage equals spokesperson effectiveness. You can't fake the first two of those three elements.

Creating Dedicated Spokesperson Roles

The most forward-thinking companies are creating hybrid roles that combine deep expertise with communication responsibility. Think of a chief public health officer at a pharmaceutical company during a health crisis or a senior director of AI ethics applications at a tech company facing an algorithm controversy.

These aren't PR people with technical training; they're technical people with communications skills and dedicated time to engage externally. The credibility is unassailable because the expertise is real.

BUILDING YOUR EXTERNAL ADVOCATE ECOSYSTEM BEFORE CRISIS HITS

As you build up your roster of external advocates, look for individuals who bring the levels of technical expertise and credibility your stakeholders and the public will embrace. Depending on your industry, you'll likely find them working in academia and think tanks, industry associations and groups, the government, and the community.

Academic and Think Tank Partners

- University researchers who can speak to broader industry issues
- Think tank experts who understand policy implications
- Former regulators who know how the system actually works

Industry Associations and Trade Groups

- Trade associations that speak for entire industries
- Professional organizations that set standards and best practices
- Supply chain partners who understand your operations
- Customer organizations that benefit from your products or services

Government Relations Network

- Current regulators who oversee your industry
- Former officials who understand how policy gets made
- Congressional staff who draft relevant legislation
- State and local officials in communities where you operate

Community Stakeholders

- Local leaders in communities with your operations
- Nonprofit partners you support or collaborate with
- Employee representatives who can speak to workplace culture
- Customer advocates who genuinely use and value your products

Increasingly, experts are developing their own media profiles and platforms. Do not write off influencers who have genuine credibility in their space. Their audiences only provide additional benefit in cases where your objectives align.

Develop Your Relationship Investment Strategy in Advance

Building a robust external advocate network requires consistent engagement well before a crisis ensues. Regularly communicate with your would-be allies and advocates, ideally by finding ways to add value to their endeavors. Go out of your way to add value. Share your expertise and insights with them when you can. Make a point of understanding their priorities and concerns, and show up for their events and support their causes. The more you authentically show up for others and can build a relationship based on genuine shared interests, the more likely it is that they will already be in your court when you need to call on them for support. These relationships can be particularly helpful when dealing with regulators. New regulations or villainization have the ability to cause irreparable harm to your business. To shore up your defenses, you'll need to create a strategy that cultivates relationships with experts and advocates who can come to your aid—both substantively and strategically—and ensure that you have allies to help respond to any negative developments in situations in which you can't be an effective messenger without looking conflicted. When it comes to protecting your company from laws and regulations that can alter the course of your business, the relationships you don't invest in could ultimately cost you everything.

The goal isn't to procure blind defenders; it's to cultivate credible voices who know you well enough to speak authentically about your character and capabilities when it matters. Start building these relationships now. Once you're embroiled in a crisis, it's too late to begin this kind of outreach.

LEVERAGING AI AS A FORCE MULTIPLIER

AI can accelerate spokesperson strategies significantly. While we'll explore the organizational implications of AI in more detail in chapter 13, it's important to note that you'll still want to rely on human voices in critical moments. As Samantha Stark explains, "ChatGPT will tell you things like, 'you need to call this person' or 'this statement should be generated from this other person.' AI will alert you to a level five situation." AI has been programmed to understand all your inputs and make the fast connections you need. It can be invaluable in its capacity to accelerate human intelligence to match the speed of the crisis you're facing. But Stark adds that you should never rely completely on AI for human judgment, especially in a crisis situation.

Key Learnings:

Crisis communication success requires four elements working in harmony:

1. Control the narrative by consciously casting the dramatic roles yourself; don't let others do it for you.
2. Make the news (or don't) through deliberate sound-bite strategy and phrase discipline.
3. Match messenger to moment *and* medium; credibility, context, and channel all matter.
4. Invest in external validators before a crisis hits; your best spokespeople might not be on payroll.

Master these four elements, and you'll do more than just survive a crisis; you'll be able to use the crisis to demonstrate exactly who you are and what you stand for. Fail at any one of them, and even the best crisis plan becomes nothing more than expensive theater where you lose control of the casting and the script.

The choices are yours, so choose deliberately. Because when you're in crisis, the audience is always watching.

CHAPTER ELEVEN

CREATE COMPELLING CONTENT; MEASURE WHAT MATTERS; IGNORE THE NOISE

By the time a crisis hits, most companies make one critical mistake: They let fear drive their decisions instead of data. I've watched executives panic over viral social media posts that had zero impact on their actual stakeholders while ignoring quiet but dangerous shifts in sentiment among the audiences that actually mattered. The companies that get blindsided are the ones flying on instinct when their competitors are operating with precision.

The organizations that emerge stronger from crises don't just survive the storm; they use data to turn it into a competitive advantage. While their rivals scramble to respond to every piece of criticism, smart leaders use measurement systems to separate real threats from noise. They know which platforms their key stakeholders actually use, what messaging moves the needle, and when silence is the strongest response. That's not just crisis management; that's crisis leverage.

The key is creating a solid content playbook and then knowing when to expand it and when to pull back from the fray.

EXPANDING YOUR PLAYBOOK

I was talking with Erika Trombley, who served in President Biden's administration as the first White House director of consumer media. She was hired by Biden's head of communications, Ben LaBolt, to help senior administration officials think differently about where real people actually get their information and how to reach them.

She told me that when she'd try to steer senior officials toward broader platforms, such as NerdWallet, the pushback could be intense. There were times when they listened, but other times, she would get laughed out of the room when she advocated for a platform with less prestige. "This is serious policy," they'd say. "It belongs in *Bloomberg*."

So, she brought the data. And she was exactly right. NerdWallet, believe it or not, has a larger reach than *Bloomberg*. Not by much, but bigger all the same.

And if their goal was to reach everyday people with practical information—how to file taxes or how the Inflation Reduction Act affects your finances—they would be missing a real opportunity by not listening to her. The folks they needed to reach aren't paying for *Bloomberg*. But they can find what they're looking for on NerdWallet. Or sometimes they'll get a push alert to their phone from their *Yahoo! Finance* app. Or they'll find out from a blogger while they scroll.

So, if you're a communicator counseling your leaders, or if you are the leader, pay attention to where the people you're trying to reach actually are. Platforms that used to define the conversation don't hold the same power they once did. And the platforms that do? They're not always going to be the ones in your playbook.

CONSIDER THE SHRINKING ATTENTION ECONOMY

The format challenge goes beyond platform selection. You're going to have to take your audience's attention span into account.

I talked to an employee communications leader at a global hospitality company who described how a significant subset of her company's employees responded well when her team evolved certain stories from intranet news articles to a more in-depth audio podcast format. Others, however, complained about the length of the podcast segments and pushed for the addition of a still recorded "news in one minute" format. It was a huge hit. Not long ago, she began receiving employee feedback that one minute is too long.

This isn't just an internal communications problem. It reflects the broader attention economy. And it matters a lot during a crisis. In a crisis situation, damaging information or misinformation is typically packaged to go viral: short, punchy, emotionally provocative content designed for maximum spread. Organizations need to keep up with this format evolution or risk losing the narrative battle before they even know they're in the fight.

Generative AI can help here, as it allows organizations to create content across multiple formats rapidly, turning a single key message into a press release, social media posts, employee talking points, and video scripts simultaneously.

If you can find a way to weave a powerful human story into the mix, you'll be on your way to producing content that packs the kind of powerful punch that will capture the hearts and minds of your target audience.

LEVERAGE THE DRAMATIC POWER OF HUMAN STORIES

Ukrainian President Volodymyr Zelenskyy understands the dramatic power of putting a human face to a story better than most leaders of his generation. By February 2023, as Ukraine approached a full year into its war with Russia, he had secured pledges of aid from Western powers and was close to getting a major $500 million commitment from the United States. But outmanned and outgunned, he knew his troops needed more than weapons. They needed hope.

On February 20, President Joe Biden took a nearly ten-hour train ride from Poland into the heart of Kyiv to stand next to Zelenskyy and present a unified front to the world. As *The New York Times* reported, "the two stepped out into the streets of Kyiv even as an air-raid siren sounded."[72]

Biden's words could have been delivered safely from the White House. But saying them on the ground in Kyiv, standing side by side with Zelenskyy in an active war zone while air-raid sirens sounded, sent a message that transcended any press release.

People need dramatic examples to shake them out of apathy. Sometimes, the greatest impact comes from simple acts, such as a humbled leader speaking authentically or a symbolic action that demonstrates commitment. The same applies to corporate crisis communication. You need that symbolic moment, the human element that helps people understand not just what happened but why it matters and what you're willing to risk to make it right.

---

72 Marc Santora, Peter Baker, and Michael D. Shear, "Biden Visits Embattled Ukraine as Air-Raid Siren Sounds," *New York Times*, February 20, 2023, https://www.nytimes.com/2023/02/20/us/politics/biden-ukraine-visit.html.

ACCESSIBILITY: MEETING EACH AUDIENCE WHERE THEY ARE READY TO RECEIVE INFORMATION

Different subsets of your various audiences need different content formats. This is especially true in a crisis, when you're competing against viral misinformation that's been optimized for engagement.

Effective communicators understand that they need multiple formats. Lulu Cheng Meservey's masterful handling of communications around a complex acquisition exemplifies this direct, unfiltered approach. During her time leading communications for Activision Blizzard, she didn't wait around for reporters to shape the narrative. As the company came under scrutiny during its proposed acquisition by Microsoft, she took to social media to post legal filings, translate dense arguments into plain English, and deliver sharp, unapologetic commentary.

Meservey famously tagged the Federal Trade Commission (FTC) in a tweet about the success of HBO's hit adaptation of the PlayStation game *The Last of Us*, chiding the FTC that game industry competition was alive and well and didn't need the government's help. The post was viewed over a million times and picked up by *Axios* and others.[73]

In many instances, Meservey laid out Activision's position with more clarity and punch than most of the headlines covering the deal. Whether you agreed with her tone or not—it could often be abrasive—she did what far too many communications leaders fail to do in a crisis: She made sure her side was heard, fast and unfiltered.

But this wasn't just social media posting; it was strategic communications warfare. Meservey understood that in the age of fractured

---

73 Stephen Totilo, "Interview: Embattled Activision Blizzard Plans to Be More Outspoken," *Axios*, February 9, 2023, https://www.axios.com/2023/02/09/activision-blizzard-lulu-cheng-meservey.

narratives and viral misinformation, waiting for someone else to tell your story is no longer a luxury that communicators can afford.

The companies that win today are the ones that move first, speak clearly, and take control of the frame before someone else does it for them.

Don't risk losing public opinion because you don't offer people the content in a manner that they're ready and willing to receive. Match the format to the audience's preferred consumption method, even if it's outside your organization's comfort zone.

And once you get your formats in sync with each audience, set up a solid measuring mechanism to validate your approach and to help you pivot when required.

MEASURE OFTEN AND ACT WITH COURAGE

A cornerstone of effective crisis communications is developing the organizational and personal resilience required to weather scrutiny. That takes the ability to effectively measure outcomes. And perhaps even more importantly, it requires the courage to act on data rather than feelings.

As a CCO or business leader, your goal shouldn't be to just build a measurement system; it needs to go way beyond that. Your goal should be to build a decision-making culture powered by the same data infrastructure that drives winning political campaigns. This isn't theoretical; it's a proven approach that my BPI colleagues and I use with Fortune 500 clients to separate signal from noise and empower bold action through data confidence.

The Political Campaign Model: What Corporate Communications Can Learn

Most companies are familiar with quantitative research, including reputation scores, sentiment tracking, and share of voice metrics. But in a crisis moment, it's important to combine it with qualitative research (e.g., focus groups, open-ended surveys, or stakeholder interviews).

This is exactly what political campaigns have been doing for decades. They don't just track overall approval ratings; they dig into why specific voter segments feel the way they do and, more importantly, what messages will actually move those voters.

Quantitative data tells you the what: "Our audience sentiment scores dropped fifteen points after the product recall announcement." Qualitative research reveals the why and, crucially, the path forward: "Customers weren't just upset about the defect; they felt blindsided by learning about it through media coverage rather than directly from us. Focus groups show that transparent, proactive communication could restore trust and potentially recover eight to ten points of lost sentiment within ninety days."

Political campaign leaders understand that message testing isn't optional; it's survival. They test every major message, every spokesperson, and every format before deployment. Corporate communications should adopt the same rigor.

A Useful Campaign-Style Framework for Corporate Communicators

1. Map Reputation Outcomes to Business Outcomes (Like Campaigns Map Polling to Electoral Math)

Political campaigns don't care about generic approval ratings; they care about approval among likely voters in swing districts. Similarly, corporate comms pros need to start by understanding which reputation metrics actually correlate with business performance. For a B2B company, this might be trust scores among procurement professionals. For a consumer brand, it could be purchase intent among its core demographic.

2. Clarify Objectives Based on Stakeholder Priority (Like Campaigns Prioritize Persuadable Voters)

Political campaigns don't try to persuade everyone; they focus on the voters who can be moved and who matter for electoral victory. Not all audiences matter equally in every corporate situation. Build a stakeholder priority map that identifies who actually has the power to impact your business in a given moment. For UTC, for example, this meant policymakers on key committees, such as the Senate Committee on Finance or the House Armed Services Committee, who controlled transportation and defense policy and funding.

3. Map Campaigns Against Objectives (Like Political Ads Target Specific Demographics)

Every piece of content, every spokesperson deployment, and every platform choice should align with specific, measurable objectives for your priority stakeholders. Political campaigns track which ads move which voter segments by how much and invest accordingly. Corporate communications should have the same precision.

4. Shift as the World Shifts (Like Campaigns Adapt to Changing Electoral Dynamics)

Political campaigns constantly adjust their strategies based on new polling data, changing news cycles, and their opponents' moves. The media landscape changes constantly. Platforms rise and fall. Audiences migrate. Your measurement framework needs to be agile enough to capture these shifts and adjust strategy accordingly.

5. Use Data to Inform Changes (Like Campaigns Make Hard Decisions Based on Numbers, Not Feelings)

Here's where courage comes in. Political campaigns kill ad campaigns that aren't working, even if the candidate loves them. They change messaging that isn't moving voters, even if it feels good to say. The data might tell you that your CEO's favorite publication doesn't actually reach your target audience. It might show that your carefully crafted message isn't resonating. You have to be willing to act on that intelligence, even when it's uncomfortable.

Build Executive Confidence Through Data Architecture

The real challenge isn't gathering the data or even interpreting the data. The real challenge you'll face will be building systems that give executives the confidence to act boldly based on that data.

Sarah Myles, director of communications measurement and insights at McDonald's, oversees reputation assessment for a brand that faces constant global scrutiny across forty thousand locations, making her framework for rapid signal assessment battle-tested at scale. She says, "To determine if a signal matters, I ask: What's the source's influence, reach, and typical engagement (ex., comments, likes, shares)? Are our stakeholders paying attention to them? Do they find the source credible? That context helps separate the signals from noise."

Aligned with Sarah's framework, I developed a decision-making grid—the traffic light decision framework—to help many of the executives and corporate communicators I work with flex their data-driven decision-making muscles in fast-moving, high-pressure situations.

The Traffic Light Decision Framework

The traffic light framework is a simple, visual system that translates complex data into clear action recommendations:

- **Red light**: A red-light scenario occurs when priority stakeholder sentiment drops below predetermined thresholds or when issue velocity indicates it will reach critical mass within twenty-four to forty-eight hours. This is your cue to take immediate action.
- **Yellow light**: In a yellow-light situation, something has occurred that warrants close and careful monitoring, but key indicators of falling stakeholder sentiment or rapid escalation of the issue haven't reached red-light levels. This is the time to prepare response materials and briefing key spokespeople, but it's not yet time to engage the public. Prepare, but don't deploy.
- **Green light**: A green-light state indicates that your current strategy is working based on stakeholder priority metrics. Stay the course.

The Schumer Test Case (Redux)

Remember the Schumer situation from chapter 9? The story our data told did not align with leadership's emotional response. Reporters weren't writing follow-ups. None of the stakeholders we cared about were engaging. No pickup. No momentum. Nothing sticky.

This was a clear yellow-light situation that leadership wanted to treat as red light because of their emotional response. The decision framework gave us language to explain to them why the best thing we could do was nothing.

The Executive Persuasion Playbook

When your data contradicts executive instincts, you need precision and authority to support data-based decisions. At BPI, our insights team, led by my colleagues Mike Schneider and Joe Ste.Marie, has been building the infrastructure to fundamentally improve how we measure communications impact and translate it into executive decision-making. Our change score measures whether content makes stakeholders feel more or less favorable toward a brand, moving beyond tone to actual reputational impact. Here's what that looks like in practice.

Where Vision Meets Risk: Mapping Your Moves

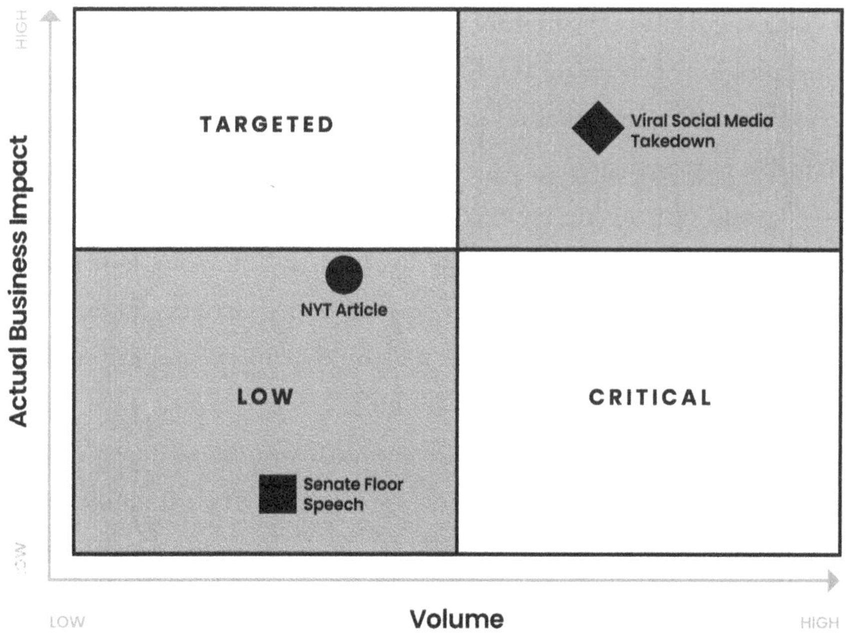

Lead with Impact, Not Volume

Emphasize that what really matters is impact and that the content you're proposing hits where it matters most. Volume doesn't produce results. Impact does. Explain how and why.

> "Using our threat matrix analysis, which plots signal versus noise, this issue ranks high on volume but low on actual business impact; it's loud, not dangerous. Here's the data on similar situations where response extended the news cycle unnecessarily."

Separate Dangerous from Loud

Show how the data indicates that feeding fuel to the story or situation could actually backfire. Just because you don't like something doesn't mean it warrants a statement or response.

Find Actual Engagement

It's easy to get lost in the noise of marketing metrics, in which millions of impressions can create the illusion of massive reach. Your job is to look past this hypothetical potential and find the sources of real, verifiable engagement.

Instead of focusing on overblown hypothetical numbers, guide leaders toward what's genuinely finding traction with your audience. This could be anything from a blog post that generates significant shares and comments to a video that holds viewers' attention far longer than a competing piece of content.

By focusing on these actual data points, you can steer the conversation toward what's truly resonating and say, "The data indicates that twelve thousand people in our core audience engaged with this message." The number may sound small compared to twenty million potential impressions, but the data is infinitely more useful.

Provide Actionable Intelligence

Show how the data provides insights around how to move forward with messaging decisions, including matters such as who should speak on the company's behalf, how to frame a statement, and what format the messaging should embrace.

"Our persuasion index shows content from [specific spokesperson] performs 40 percent better with our priority audience than CEO statements. Our backlash score flags this messaging approach as high-risk."

Format for Executive Consumption

When presenting the data and accompanying insights, focus on the visual. Keep it clean and sharp. Think bullet briefings and quadrant visuals, not spreadsheet dumps. Be clear about what your CEO and others need to know and what they can ignore. Be specific about what needs to be done. Eliminate the need for any possible "so what" questions by clarifying the significance of your data interpretation from the outset.

Practical Implementation: Four-Step Bold Decision System

Step 1: Baseline and Benchmark

- **Set the baseline**: Use audience research to measure the favorability of existing brand content and work to get an understanding of current reach. Catalogue commentary from stakeholders who actually impact your business.

Step 2: Building the Decision Dashboard

- **Deploy a real-time system**: The system should show volume over time on a platform-specific basis. Track the performance of individual pieces of content for comparison.

Step 3: Pilot Test with Leadership

- **Use proven case studies from real implementations**:
  - **Content amplification filter**: Show leadership which positive content should be amplified and which negative content poses real reputational risk.
  - **Performance analysis**: Break down executive appearances (e.g., CEO podcast interviews) to show which clips help or hurt brand perception. It often helps to show competitor performance as well for comparison.

Step 4: Full Implementation and Scaling

- **Build a repeatable system**: The system should reflect the metrics with the greatest impact, using the visualizations your colleagues respond to most. Track consistently versus periodically and build organizational familiarity with the format.

DEVELOP THICK SKIN TO BUILD RESILIENCE

Once you are confident in the data, you have to be comfortable with discomfort. This is one of the hardest challenges for a corporate board or leadership team to face.

Toughness is not traditionally a corporate strong suit, but it increasingly needs to be. The age of issues demands that leaders find their ground, are as sure as they can be that they're standing in the right place, and are then prepared to fight for their positions.

The companies that win today don't just weather storms; they use the turbulence to build stronger, more resilient operations. The companies that thrive in this environment are the ones that can take hits and keep moving forward.

The Bold Decision Accelerators

Over the years, I've observed and honed several techniques for helping leaders develop thick skin as they embrace bold decision-making. The following three have proven the most beneficial, as they build confidence by offering empirical support for a particular position, providing evidence of how competitors and stakeholders are responding in real time.

Evidence-Based Scenario Planning

This type of decision accelerator helps build confidence by showing executives how similarly situated companies have dealt with the scenario in question: "Here's what happened when [similar company] responded to [similar situation] versus when it stayed quiet."

Real-Time Competitive Intelligence

Here, data-based competitive intelligence bolsters decision-making: "Our monitoring shows competitors are getting positive traction on [specific messaging], while our approach is having limited impact. Here's the data-driven pivot recommendation."

Stakeholder-Specific Insights

Drilling down to how different stakeholders respond to your proposed strategies offers additional support: "Consumers who identify as Democrats respond differently to this content than those identifying as Republicans. Here's the platform and messaging strategy for each segment based on their actual media consumption patterns."

Stakeholder Priority Grid

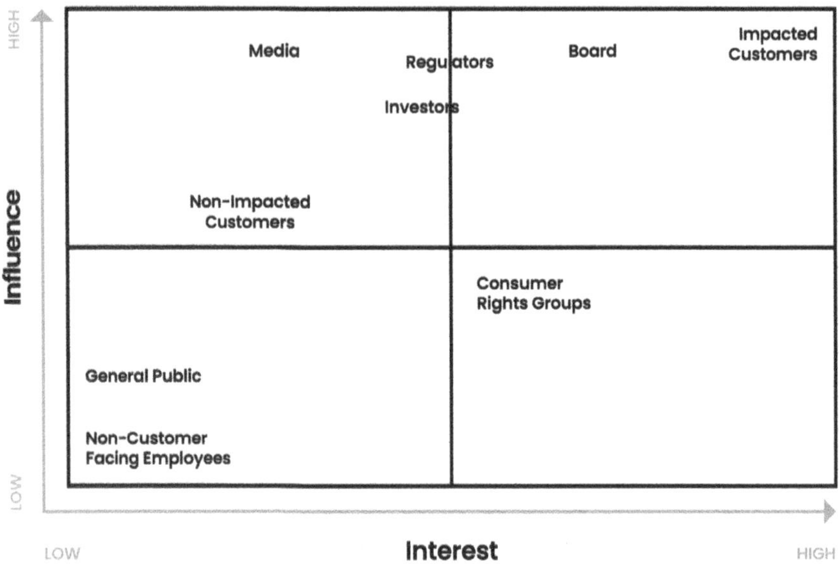

Key Learnings:

Actionable data separates companies that fight for their lives during crises from those that avoid the majority of crises before they ever get the chance to hit. While competitors scramble to respond to every piece of criticism, smart leaders use measurement systems to turn conflict into competitive advantage.

Instead of chasing vanity metrics, track actual impact. Work to understand not just what your audiences think but what will actually move them.

And remember, in today's world, thick skin isn't just helpful; it's infrastructure. Successful communicators:

- Use data to separate real threats from Twitter noise
- Make bold decisions based on evidence, not executive panic
- Focus on metrics that matter instead of trying to make everyone happy

The companies that thrive don't avoid criticism; they use data to know which battles are worth fighting.

CHAPTER TWELVE

HARNESSING THE POWER OF VULNERABILITY

HUMANIZING RESPONSES IN A WORLD THAT'S OUT FOR BLOOD

Steve Jobs never talked about gigabytes or processor speeds. He talked about putting "a thousand songs in your pocket."[74] He didn't describe tablet computers. He showed people how they could "hold the internet in their hands."

When Jobs introduced the iPhone in 2007, he didn't lead with technical specifications. He said, "Today, Apple is going to reinvent the phone."[75]

Then he paused. He let it sink in. He made everyone in the room, as well as everyone watching around the world, feel like they were witnessing history.

---

74 Steve Jobs, "iPod Introduction," All About Steve Jobs, October 23, 2001.

75 Steve Jobs, "iPhone 2007 Presentation" (transcript), Singju Post, July 2014, https://singjupost.com/wp-content/uploads/2014/07/Steve-Jobs-iPhone-2007-Presentation-Full-Transcript.pdf.

That wasn't an accident. That was masterful communication. Jobs recognized what most CEOs miss completely: People don't connect with features and benefits. They connect with possibility. They connect with vision. They connect with leaders who can articulate not just what they're building but why it matters to our lives.

Jobs understood the fundamental truth that people don't buy what you make. They buy why you make it. And they definitely don't connect with corporate speak. People connect with vision, with possibility, with the feeling that your company understands something important about their lives. This is what authentic leadership communications is about—connecting your company's mission to something that matters deeply to the people who need to believe in it.

And when a crisis hits, people connect with authenticity.

THE MOMENT CORPORATE ARMOR CRACKS

Picture the room: a corporate training facility, fluorescent lights, and the smell of burnt coffee. Seated across the table is a six-foot-two, intimidating operations executive known throughout the company as the guy who never breaks.

My BPI business partner at the time, former Obama White House Press Secretary Robert Gibbs, and I were there to prepare this executive and his team for a major press briefing. We're talking *The New York Times*, *The Wall Street Journal*, *The Washington Post*, *Bloomberg*—all there to hear him review our client's progress on safety improvements after a fatal product incident. We'd been through hours of practice, and most of his responses had been borderline smug. Technically accurate and legally defensible, but completely forgettable.

Then I pressed him: "Do you even think about the people who lost their lives as a result of your product? Do you think about their families?"

Silence.

After what felt like an eternity, Gibbs leaned forward: "Help us understand why this matters to you."

The executive's composure cracked. He sighed as tears began to roll down his face.

"Not a day goes by that I don't think about what we could have done differently," he said, his voice barely above a whisper. "It fuels my commitment to ensure something like this can never happen again."

It was the most believable thing any executive at that company had said since the crisis began.

We completely reoriented the briefing strategy around that moment of vulnerability. Instead of hiding behind technical details and legal disclaimers, we led with the human element. The coverage that followed, which should have been a brutal grilling, was neutral to positive.

Authenticity is disarming. When someone speaks from genuine emotion rather than corporate scripting, it's almost impossible not to believe them.

The leaders we respect and celebrate most, particularly in a crisis, are the ones we consider authentic. Not perfect. Not polished. Not programmed by their legal departments.

Human.

Yet most companies operate from the opposite position. They default to robot mode. They speak in a passive voice. They hide behind carefully crafted statements that say nothing while covering everything. They prioritize liability avoidance over human connection.

Here's what they're missing: When everyone has a platform and no one trusts institutions, authenticity isn't just nice to have. It's survival.

DAMAR HAMLIN AND THE NFL'S MASTER CLASS IN HUMANITY

On January 2, 2023, during *Monday Night Football*, Buffalo Bills safety Damar Hamlin suffered cardiac arrest on the field after what appeared to be a routine tackle. For nineteen terrifying minutes, medical personnel worked to save his life while millions watched in stunned silence. The NFL made a decision it hadn't made since 1935: It postponed the game and never replayed it.

What followed turned out to be a master class in crisis communications under one of the most emotionally charged circumstances imaginable.

Katie Hill, a former comms director for Obama who now serves as the NFL's senior vice president of communications, was deeply involved in orchestrating the League's response. Her account reveals how an organization managed one of the most-watched crises in sports history while never losing sight of what mattered most: a young man fighting for his life.

"The first thing was centering Damar in his experience and making sure that no one ever—journalists and fans and other players—lost sight of the fact that we were talking about a young man who for several days we didn't know if he was going to live or not," Hill explains.

When conversations began shifting to broader topics, including the dangers of the game, how long it took to postpone, and scheduling implications, the NFL's communications team consistently redirected the focus back to what mattered. This wasn't about protecting the brand. It was about protecting a person.

This choice set the entire narrative frame. Every subsequent decision flowed from this core principle: Damar's life and recovery came first, everything else second.

The challenge was reacting to and managing the needs of a universe of stakeholders. "You've got fans, you've got sponsors and partners. You've got thirty-two teams, thirty-two owners. You have League office employees, and we have three offices domestically and a number of smaller offices internationally. Players—hugely important constituency. The players union—hugely important constituency," Hill states.

Each group had different needs, different concerns, and different information requirements. The crisis was managed "hour by hour, sometimes minute by minute," with the team "going through each of them and saying, what are we hearing from them? Who has been in touch? What are we saying to them when? And then figuring out the order of operations."

The sequencing was everything. As Katie says, "You don't want owners and players reading about something for the first time in an article. That can certainly inflame things."

Process Under the Microscope

Hill's Washington background proved invaluable in managing the complexity. She drew much of her playbook from her experiences at the White House and later as Obama's post-presidential comms director: "You can't have world-class outcomes without world-class process. Even something as simple as you accidentally leave somebody off of an email can have catastrophic consequences in a crisis."

The NFL's response required surgical precision in stakeholder management. Internal communications had to happen before external statements. Key constituencies needed to be briefed before press conferences. Every sequence mattered.

Information Control in Real Time

Hill knew that managing medical information requires especially careful coordination. The League carved out lanes very early on about what the league office would speak to and what it would leave to the medical experts. "We really relied on the subject matter experts and determined in advance what the Buffalo Bills would speak to and what the experts at the University of Cincinnati Medical Center would speak to—the ones who are actually treating Damar."

This became crucial, as Hill explained that "very quickly, when it comes to medical crises, you get the Twitter physicians, the armchair docs. Cable news has an imperative to fill a twenty-four-hour news cycle, and it's easy to do that with well-credentialed physicians who are going to offer opinions despite not having seen the patient, let alone treated him."

The strategy was to consistently redirect the conversation to the experts with responses such as "This is one person's opinion who actually is not treating Damar, so you should really be going to the University of Cincinnati doctors."

Choosing Your Battles

The inevitable conspiracy theories emerged. "There was a conspiracy theory that Damar had actually died, and that it was a body double who had left the hospital. It's just really awful, insidious stuff. That reached a level where we felt like we had to bat that down," Hill explained. But she was still strategic about which fights to pick: "You choose your spots, because if you're out there all day long swatting away rumors, then you dilute your own voice."

The NFL learned that not every piece of misinformation deserves a response. But when false narratives threaten core facts, such as whether someone is alive or dead, you have to act decisively.

Crisis as a Catalyst for Good

The NFL refused to let tragedy be the end of the story: "We try not to let a good crisis go to waste in the sense of how do you take a moment that was quite dark and use our platform for good. Damar felt the same way. He wanted to use what had happened to him for good. We joined with him and founded the Smart Heart Sports Coalition with the other major sports leagues and the American Heart Association to push for stronger laws in all fifty states to improve access to AEDs."

This transformation wasn't just about messaging; it was about action. The foundation of the League's success became its core message: "What saved Damar's life that night was that there was an emergency action plan in place. At every stadium there is a run-through before every single NFL game, so that every member knows what they're supposed to do in a medical emergency. Because that's drilled and drilled and drilled, Damar is still with us today."

THE NEW RULES IN ACTION

Hamlin not only survived but returned to football, making his first start since the incident in September 2024. More importantly, his story sparked nationwide CPR education, with the NFL investing over $1 million in related programs.

The NFL's Hamlin response offers a crisis management blueprint: When the stakes are highest, humanity wins. By refusing to hide behind corporate speak, maintaining obsessive focus on process, and transforming a near-tragedy into a force for good, the League turned its darkest moment into one of its finest.

The lesson isn't just about sports; it's about leadership in an age when authenticity matters more than polish, stakeholders demand transparency over control, and the organizations that thrive are those that remember crises are about people, not just PR.

When everything stops, what you do next defines who you are.

THE WEIGHT OF REAL LOSS: MICHAEL STUMO AND NADIA MILLERON

In crisis situations, the stakes can be extremely high. And unlike in Damar Hamlin's case, not everyone always survives.

I think constantly about Michael Stumo and Nadia Milleron, who lost their daughter Samya on Ethiopian Airlines Flight 302, a Boeing 737 MAX. Even though I wasn't at the company at the time of the crashes, their stories weighed heavily on me. They've campaigned vulnerably and passionately against the company, demanding answers, accountability, and change.

During a personal conversation after my tenure with Boeing, someone made a joke about the Stumos "being at it again" after one of their particularly incendiary news conferences. I flipped out.

> **"We never make light of this situation or these people. No one should ever go through what they have been through."**

There are nights when I still cry involuntarily, thinking about the pain that family and so many others have to live with. As uncomfortable as that feeling is, I embrace it.

Some people don't want to know the names of those impacted by crises they're involved in. They don't want to humanize them, because it makes it harder to defend your organization when you know the victims' stories. I've always felt that's a mistake.

You're not credible or believable when you defend your actions or talk about change unless you've truly worked to understand the consequences of failing to improve. The toll it takes on people's lives. The surprising amount you have in common with those impacted. The unshakable feeling of knowing it could have just as easily been you or your family.

You're not credible or believable when you defend your actions or talk about change unless you've truly worked to understand the consequences of failing to improve.

The point isn't to create guilt. It's to give you a filter through which to evaluate your actions and your language. Do the steps you're taking go far enough? Are the words you're using direct enough? Compassionate enough?

This isn't about choosing sides in some corporate narrative battle. It's about recognizing that we're all real people. Your company can be making genuine improvements at the same time that victims of your product's malfunction hate you and try to burn you down.

Being human means accepting it all, respecting it all, and making space for it all.

Allowing yourself to be vulnerable doesn't make you weak; it gives you the strength and ammunition to insist on a response that meets the moment as if it were you or someone you cared about on the other side.

THE CORPORATE TENDENCY TOWARD ROBOTICS

Most companies approach crisis communications like they're diffusing a bomb. Every word gets vetted by legal. Every statement gets stripped of emotion. Every human element gets sanitized away. Their default mode is liability avoidance.

The result? Communications that sound like they were written by an algorithm for an audience of lawyers.

- **Robot version**: "The company takes these matters seriously and is committed to reviewing our processes to ensure compliance with industry standards and regulatory requirements."
- **Human version**: "We messed up. People were hurt. We're fixing it. Here's how."

Which one would you trust?

The truth is, it's natural to want to hide behind legal language. It feels safer. But in times of uncertainty and fear, people want leadership, not legalese. That goes for words and for actions. The leaders we remember aren't those who avoided difficult moments but those who rose to meet them with genuine humanity. Anita McBride, who served as chief of staff to First Lady Laura Bush, witnessed this firsthand during one of America's darkest hours.

"There are things you can't plan for, and how you respond to those is a real test of leadership. 9/11 happens—who could plan for something like that? You go from a domestic-focused administration to a nation at war in nine months. The big test when you're in these positions is, how do you respond? You have to draw from your own inner reserves to rise to a level of responsibility you could not have predicted."

This isn't just about crisis management; it's about character. When everything you thought you knew gets stripped away, what remains is who you really are and what you truly stand for. The organizations that thrive in crisis aren't those led by people with perfect plans but by those with authentic conviction and the vulnerability to admit when they're facing something entirely new.

AUTHENTICITY AS STRATEGY: MCDONALD'S "WE ARE GOLDEN"

During the 2024 presidential election cycle, McDonald's found itself in an increasingly politicized spotlight. Both candidates had been drawing on the McDonald's name and affiliation to score political points throughout their campaigns. When Trump visited a Pennsylvania location during the campaign's final stretch, McDonald's faced a defining moment.

It could have issued a standard corporate nonstatement. Instead, it chose to reset the narrative with a message rooted in its core values:

"McDonald's does not endorse candidates for elected office. We are not red or blue—we are golden."

The memo acknowledged the broader context: "As we've seen, our brand has been a fixture of conversation this election cycle. While we've not sought this, it's a testament to how much McDonald's resonates with so many Americans."

Then, McDonald's backed it up with action, noting it had also invited Vice President Harris and Governor Walz to visit locations "in order to share how McDonald's provides meaningful pathways to economic opportunity and feeds and fosters local communities."[76]

76 "Read McDonald's Memo About Trump's Controversial Visit: 'We Are Not Red or Blue—We Are Golden,'" Quartz, October 22, 2024, https://qz.com/mcdonalds-donald-trump-visit-memo-fryer-fast-food-1851678163.

The result? Rather than allowing itself to be pulled into a partisan narrative, McDonald's used the moment to reinforce its brand identity. It transformed potential controversy into affirmation of its values.

REV. JESSE JACKSON: WHEN LEADERSHIP COMMUNICATIONS TRANSFORM LIVES

"I am somebody!"

Three simple words that Rev. Jesse Jackson shouted to crowds during his groundbreaking 1984 and 1988 presidential campaigns. The first time I heard them in person as a young staffer twenty years later at Rev. Jackson's Rainbow PUSH Coalition, they felt silly. I didn't want to say them out loud. But by the fourth or fifth call, I was shouting them back, and I realized how desperately I needed to hear myself say them.

Rev. Jackson's campaigns were revolutionary, not just politically but communicatively. He wasn't running to simply win; he was running to prove that someone who looked like him, who came from where he came from, could stand on the same stage as anyone and be taken seriously. His message to disenfranchised communities across America was radical in its simplicity: You matter. Your voice counts. You belong at this table.

But here's what made Rev. Jackson's approach so powerful. He didn't just tell people they mattered; he showed them. When he spotted a wide-eyed student at Northwestern University who had the passion to grab him by the shoulder after a press conference about flying to Iran to negotiate the release of BBC journalist Roxana Saberi, he didn't just listen. He gave that kid a platform. That kid was me. Less than a month later, I was speaking on his international broadcast as the campaign manager and student face of Reduce the Rate, his push for college affordability and access.

THE GESTURE THAT DEFINED LEADERSHIP

Years later, Rev. Jackson demonstrated what authentic leadership looks like in the smallest moments. I was supposed to meet my then-girlfriend for a date after a meeting with Rwanda's president ran hours long. I looked mortified.

"What's going on, buddy?" Rev. Jackson asked.

I explained the situation. He offered his driver, but I'd missed the date by hours. All I could do was call to apologize, but my phone was dead. In an act of pure generosity, he handed me his own cell phone.

I called, but it went straight to voicemail. Defeated, I called my mom instead to tell her I was OK, since the news showed protesters outside our meeting.

As soon as the reverend saw me talking to someone, he snatched the phone back, thinking it was my girlfriend. "This is Jesse Jackson. Please don't be mad at Bradley; he makes his share of mistakes, but this time, it's my fault. He was just helping me out."

He handed me the phone back with a wink. My mother was speechless. I never escaped the doghouse with my girlfriend, but I'll never forget Rev. Jackson's gesture.

I worked hard for Rev. Jackson because he fought the little battles just as passionately as the big ones. The fierce loyalty I developed was forged in moments like these.

For business leaders, it's these moments that reveal the deepest truth about authentic communications. Your brand as an employer isn't about what you offer people. It's about how people see themselves when they work for you. Do they feel empowered? Heard? Valued? Do they believe that their voice matters and that this is the table where they belong?

Rev. Jackson's "I am somebody" wasn't just a slogan; it was a management philosophy. He created a culture where everyone understood their worth. That internal authenticity became the foundation for communications that changed American politics forever.

THE CATCH-22 OF AUTHENTICITY: WHEN BEING REAL COMES AT A COST

Jackson's "I am somebody" wasn't just a slogan; it was a management philosophy. He created a culture where everyone understood their worth.

Authenticity sounds great in theory. In practice, it's messy and risky, especially for leaders who don't fit traditional expectations.

The challenge for minority leaders is even more complex. As I've written before, most notably in *Forbes*, authenticity often represents a higher risk when you're the only one, or one of the few people like you, at your level. There's pressure to prove you belong by conforming to existing expectations rather than bringing your full self to work.

The lesson isn't to avoid authenticity. It's to understand the stakes and choose your moments wisely.

And there's another ugly truth that this moment demands we reckon with: The stakes of stating your opinion in America have become unacceptably high.

I've spent my career helping leaders navigate crises, and I've learned that authenticity matters, but so does safety. Show up authentically, yes. But also protect your safety and the safety of others. Because no victory, no perfect sound bite, is worth paying the ultimate price.

Conservative activist Charlie Kirk's killing followed the assassination of Minnesota House Speaker Melissa Hortman and UnitedHealthcare CEO Brian Thompson just months before. Different motivations, different ideologies, same horrific outcome.

Every spokesperson, public figure, and leader needs to think about this reality. We now operate in an environment where speaking publicly comes with physical risk. Security isn't just for presidents and celebrities. It's a consideration for anyone who steps into the public square with a microphone and a message. Be thoughtful.

Authenticity as Offense (How Bob Iger Reclaimed Disney's Soul)

When Bob Chapek succeeded Bob Iger as Disney's CEO in 2020, he inherited the Magic Kingdom but not the magic. Iger had mastered narrative leadership and embodied Disney's values. When Chapek's pandemic decisions felt cold and his communications lacked warmth, Iger remained in the background, occasionally issuing statements that reinforced Disney's values-driven identity. *Chapek had the title. Iger had the trust.*

Less than three years later, Disney's board asked Iger to return, a restoration of Disney's soul through authentic leadership.

The Ed Blum Playbook: How to Weaponize Sympathetic Stories

Conservative activist Ed Blum never went to Harvard or the University of North Carolina. He's not Asian American. By any traditional measure, he had no standing to challenge affirmative action at America's most prestigious universities.

But Blum understood something that most corporate communicators miss: In the battle for public opinion, the most sympathetic story wins. Always.

The Strategic Setup

For his final assault on affirmative action—the cases that would ultimately reach the Supreme Court—Blum orchestrated a symphony of narrative warfare.

His plaintiffs weren't faceless legal arguments. They were real students with compelling personal stories. Asian American applicants who'd been rejected despite exceptional test scores and grades. Students who felt they'd been penalized for their race. Students whose parents had immigrated to America believing that merit alone would determine their children's futures.

Students for Fair Admissions v. Harvard,[77] the lead case on affirmative action in college admissions that eventually reached the Supreme Court, wasn't really about legal precedent. It was about *narrative frames.* Blum cast his plaintiffs as victims of institutional discrimination. He positioned Harvard as an elite gatekeeper perpetuating systemic unfairness. And he framed affirmative action not as a remedy for historical injustice but as reverse racism against hardworking families.

The Communications Genius

Blum didn't need to win every argument. He just needed to win the most important one: *Who deserves sympathy?*

By casting his plaintiffs as victims rather than beneficiaries of privilege, he flipped the traditional civil rights narrative. The media

---

77 *Students for Fair Admissions v. Harvard*, 600 U.S. 181 (2023).

coverage followed predictably. Every story included sympathetic profiles of rejected applicants. The human face of opposition to affirmative action became young, diverse, and undeniably sympathetic.

In June 2023, the Supreme Court ruled 6–3 against Harvard and the University of North Carolina, effectively ending affirmative action in college admissions. Blum had demonstrated how carefully selected and strategically deployed authentic human stories can dismantle institutional policies that seemed untouchable.

The Corporate Warning

Blum's success carries a crucial lesson for business leaders: *Your opponents are already using authentic stories against you.* Labor organizers share worker testimonials. Environmental activists highlight community health impacts. Consumer advocates amplify customer complaints.

If you're not equally strategic about authentic storytelling, you're playing defense in a game where offense wins.

Blum's playbook works because it's based on a fundamental truth: People trust individual stories more than institutional statements. When someone shares their personal pain or struggle, our instinct is to believe them. When an organization shares carefully crafted messaging, our instinct is to question its motives.

You have a choice. Keep relying on corporate communications that no one believes. Or start collecting and sharing the authentic human stories that prove your organization's value. Because if you don't tell those stories, someone else will tell different ones about you, and theirs will probably win.

PRACTICAL APPLICATIONS: HOW TO HUMANIZE YOUR COMMUNICATIONS

1. Lead with Values, Not Vulnerabilities

Don't mistake authenticity for emotional oversharing. The goal isn't to cry in public. It's to speak from a place of genuine conviction about what matters to your organization. Before any crisis, identify your nonnegotiable values. When pressure mounts, those values become your North Star.

2. Use Concrete Details, Not Corporate Speak

Authenticity lives in specifics. Instead of "We are committed to implementing enhanced safety protocols," try "We've changed three specific things: our training program, our maintenance schedule, and our reporting process. Here's exactly what each one means."

3. Match Your Messenger to Your Message

The right spokesperson isn't always the CEO. It's whoever can deliver the message most credibly to your specific audience. During the Hamlin crisis, the NFL's various voices served different purposes, each authentic to its role.

4. Embrace Strategic Vulnerability

There's a difference between being vulnerable and being weak. Strategic vulnerability means acknowledging uncertainty, mistakes, or emotions when doing so builds rather than undermines credibility.

INTERNAL COMMUNICATIONS: THE HIDDEN ENGINE

Your communications strategy directly affects your ability to attract and retain talent. Recent BPI research revealed that 54 percent of employees are thinking about quitting, and 49 percent say official communications don't address what's really going on at their organizations. Only 22 percent always open company-wide emails.[78] If employees aren't convinced they're better off working for you, they're going to make you pay a premium to keep them.

Steve Jobs didn't just communicate with finesse to the public about products; he also knew how to communicate with Apple's employees. His internal presentations were just as visionary as his public keynotes. He communicated the same way to his employees as he did to the press. He knew that when leadership communicate authentically, they attract a workforce that show up not just for a paycheck but because they believe in what is being built together.

Key Learnings

In today's fractured media landscape, authenticity serves dual purposes:

- **Offense**: Authentic narratives can reshape entire industries, movements, or markets. Think Rev. Jackson's presidential campaigns, Iger's Disney comeback, or the NFL's transformation of the Hamlin crisis into a force for good.

78 Akubuiro, "The Surprising Thing Your Employees Still Believe."

- **Defense:** When a crisis hits, authentic leaders who've built trust can weather storms that would destroy their more polished competitors.

The Bottom Line for CEOs

Your legal team will always counsel caution. Your board might prefer bland statements. Your PR agency might default to corporate speak.

Ignore them.

Not because they're wrong about the risks. But because in today's world, the biggest risk is being ignored entirely. At a time when everyone has a platform and no one trusts institutions, the only way to break through is to speak like a human being to other human beings.

The companies that thrive won't be the ones with the best lawyers. They'll be the ones with the most authentic leaders. The choice is yours. Either keep reading from the script your team hands you or start speaking from the heart about what actually matters.

One approach protects you from lawsuits. The other preserves your license to operate.

Choose wisely.

CHAPTER THIRTEEN

PUT STAKEHOLDERS FIRST

HOW TO DESIGN ORGS FOR TRUST

As important as building systems that can withstand crises is, designing organizations that are responsive to the environment we're in is more valuable. The current landscape has fundamentally changed CEOs' expectations of communications leaders. As I wrote in a column for PRovoke Media in 2022, "CEOs are increasingly looking for a single leader on their teams to turn to for guidance—leaders with an informed point of view who can help counsel them credibly and holistically on how to maneuver these matters both internally and externally."[79]

They're no longer looking for strategic comms leaders; they're seeking strategic business consiglieres who can navigate the intersection of policy, culture, and reputation. Titles such as chief corporate affairs officer designate strategic integration. These roles typically consolidate communications, government affairs, and corporate giving

79 Bradley Akubuiro, "The Age of the Impact Officer & What It Means for Comms," PRovoke Media, March 3, 2022, https://www.provokemedia.com/latest/article/the-age-of-the-impact-officer-what-it-means-for-comms.

under unified leadership. For communications professionals, this represents both an opportunity and an imperative: expand beyond traditional comms and media relations into policy fluency, specialized audience insight, and reputation metrics that actually matter to business outcomes.

This is true during crisis, and also true of communications in general—audience-aligned organizations move faster and with more precision than those built any other way.

I have addressed the systems for understanding your stakeholders in previous chapters, but this chapter is about restructuring your organization's communications function around the concept of stakeholder understanding. In the current Age of Issues, this is the smartest approach you can take.

BUILDING FROM THE STAKEHOLDER LENS

Smart organizations design their communications function from the outside in. The most effective structure is the one that's optimized to engage the stakeholders most critical to the business's success.

There are multiple models you can follow, depending on the stakeholders you prioritize. Here are a few different examples of how to consider framing based on a few of the most commonly prioritized stakeholder groups: employees, the public and civil society, and shareholders and regulators.

Employees: Managing Your Most Influential Audience

Your employees the audience most likely to see through corporate BS. During a crisis, they'll either amplify your message or undermine it. There's no middle ground.

If your own employees don't believe you, no one else will.

Most organizations make the mistake of treating internal communications as an afterthought, something to manage after the "real" communications work is done. But for organizations that recognize talent as their core asset (or their greatest liability), a people-centric model can make good sense.

Look at Visa's approach. It has unified people (HR) and corporate affairs under vice chair Kelly Tullier, creating what it calls the people and corporate affairs function. This isn't communications reporting to HR; it's strategic recognition that in high-stakes moments, your people strategy and your reputation strategy are fundamentally interconnected. When employees feel heard, protected, and aligned with the company's mission, they become your most powerful advocates.

Under Tullier's leadership, Visa maintains clear internal communication chains and has empowered messengers throughout the organization—not just senior leadership—who can translate executive messaging into language that resonates with their teams. It runs internal simulations that account for emotional and reputational impact, not just operational response.

Most importantly, Visa treats employees as the critical first audience for any public-facing message. If it doesn't work internally, it won't work externally.

More and more companies recognize the virtue of this approach. Southwest Airlines followed similar logic when then-CCO Linda Rutherford's portfolio expanded to include communications, people, IT, and other functions, driving the airline's employee culture through all touchpoints.

The logic behind the approaches undertaken by both Visa and Southwest Airlines is clear: The executive who understands how to effectively engage its employees is often best positioned to lead all of the functions charged with driving an employee-centric culture.

Public and Civil Society: Managing Narrative in a Distrustful Era

Your audience—customers, consumers, activists, community leaders—are bombarded with information and armed with skepticism.

The companies best suited to break through the noise are frequently the ones who have strategically integrated their communications and marketing functions. IBM's integrated communications and marketing model recognizes that reputation defense and brand building are two sides of the same coin. Its structure includes brand reputation managers who bridge traditional communications and marketing functions. Breaking down these walls has significant advantages for its business. You can imagine that during AI ethics discussions, IBM didn't need to separate proactive innovation messaging from reactive issues management messaging; it integrated them into a single narrative, positioning itself as both cutting-edge and responsible.

Moderna exemplifies this integration at a smaller scale. During the pandemic, its communications strategy was embedded within its clinical and policy work. It created *Coffee Break Science*: short, conversational videos that took complex vaccine science and made it accessible to general audiences. During this time of societal crisis, Moderna oriented its comms structure towards ongoing public education that built trust through consistency and clarity.

Civil society stakeholders, including NGOs, foundations, and all sorts of community leaders, have long memories and little patience for corporate virtue signaling. They want authenticity over rhetoric, action over statements. They can detect inauthenticity from orbit, and they have platforms to amplify their skepticism instantly.

Airbnb unified its global policy, communications, and crisis management teams as a single function under former White House Press Secretary Jay Carney, recognizing that when facing regulatory scrutiny, public criticism, and crisis situations simultaneously across multiple jurisdictions, the company's policy positions and public communications needed to be perfectly aligned. During regulatory battles in cities from London to São Paulo, housing policy debates, tax compliance issues, safety regulation discussions, and crisis incidents involving property damage or guest safety, Airbnb needed to speak with one voice across all markets while adapting its messaging to local regulatory environments.

To succeed with a complex, external-first orientation, you can't just be reactive; you must be anticipatory. These models reflect teams that understand how social issues might intersect with their business and are prepared to respond with nuance.

Shareholders and Regulators: Managing Risk and Restoring Confidence

In times of crisis, your formal stakeholders—regulators, investors, and boards—aren't looking for empathy. They're looking for competence. They want transparency, discipline, and a clear chain of accountability. They want to see that you understand the problem, own the solution, and have systems in place to prevent recurrence.

> *The expectation is straightforward: Show, don't tell, that you're in control.*

McDonald's approach exemplifies this integration perfectly. The chief impact officer, a role first occupied by Obama White House alum Katie Beirne Fallon and now by Jon Banner, oversees an organization that combines communications, government relations, and corporate citizenship, including community relations and corporate giving. This ensures that virtually all stakeholder-related risk, be it an incident in a local restaurant, an *E. coli* outbreak in a certain region, or a political advocacy campaign to challenge the company on minimum wage, will be tracked and addressed by a unified team in a unified voice.

Separately, the company's global crisis management standard is co-owned by the general counsel and the chief impact officer, ensuring that messaging during high-stakes incidents is both legally sound and transparently communicated from the start.

While not formalized by structure, this legal–communications collaboration prevents the paralysis that destroys credibility with formal stakeholders. The parties move quickly to take responsibility, outline specific steps for investigation and remediation, and provide regular updates that satisfy both regulatory requirements and public concern. They align their public messaging with their regulatory disclosures, avoiding credibility gaps that destroy trust.

The structural elements include defined escalation protocols with clear criteria to follow when different levels of leadership get involved. They've built crisis dashboards and key performance indicators directly into enterprise risk management systems, allowing leadership to track response effectiveness in real time.

The best practice here is to treat formal stakeholders as partners in problem-solving rather than just audiences for messaging. Structure your team to brief them early, update them regularly, and give them the information they need to support your response rather than second-guess it.

Your Integration Decision Matrix

Most reorganizations fail because leaders don't design them based on reality. Before you sketch another org chart, answer one question—where can your reputation actually break?

If your CEO will be spending half her time over the next two years managing senators who want to regulate you out of existence, integrate communications with government relations. If the war for talent is red hot in your sector or employees are walking out over culture issues, consider welding communications to HR. Companies gearing up for an IPO or a bout of major M&A may want investor relations and communications as a single unit. And if the focus is on winning back customers, communications-marketing integration might be your best path forward.

The assessment process is simple: Audit who actually owns your critical relationships today. Mark which function manages each of your top twenty stakeholders right now. If government relations controls 60 percent of the conversations that matter to your business, they should anchor everything. Organizational design isn't about theory; it's about power and relationships that already exist.

Your crisis history is more honest than any consultant's framework. Pull your last five significant issues and identify what coordination breakdowns nearly killed you. Did legal and communications work at cross-purposes while the media destroyed your narrative? Did policy and communications send contradictory signals to regulators? Those coordination failures aren't accidents—they're architecture problems screaming for structural solutions.

Pay attention to where your CEO's mind actually lives, but don't blindly follow. Your organizational design should drive where it needs to go. If regulatory risk poses your greatest business threat, integrate policy and communications—then position your CEO to spend serious time with the regulators and policymakers who control your fate. If talent retention threatens your ability to execute, fuse people and communications because you need your CEO treating culture as a reputation crisis, not an HR checkbox. Your structure isn't just reflecting current reality; it's building the machine that forces leadership to focus on what actually threatens the business.

Finally, get brutally real about whether your organization can handle this transformation. Is your executive team genuinely open to consolidation? Do your functional leaders collaborate or operate like warring fiefdoms? Do you have budget for this reorganization?

Implementation Realities: Securing Buy-In and Managing Resistance

The moment you announce a reorganization, everyone assumes they're losing something. Before any permanent change, pilot the integration. Choose one high-stakes project requiring cross-functional coordination—maybe a regulatory inquiry generating media attention, or a policy change affecting employees that needs external positioning. Document the results: decisions made faster, better stakeholder outcomes, fewer mixed messages. Use those wins to build momentum. Two things should begin to change within weeks: First, your alignment: stakeholders should start to notice your company communicating more consistently across channels. And second, your efficiency: cost per stakeholder touchpoint should drop as you eliminate duplication.

AI AS YOUR FORCE MULTIPLIER: BUILDING SMARTER, FASTER COMMUNICATIONS

Before we turn to implementation, there's one more critical element reshaping how smart organizations structure their communications functions: AI. Every company is grappling with how AI both threatens and empowers its stakeholder communications. The organizations that master this balance will have a decisive advantage.

AI enables both unprecedented threats and unprecedented capabilities.

With AI, anyone can now create convincing fake websites, clone executive voices, or generate professional-quality disinformation campaigns. But the inverse is also true. AI can be a force for transformative opportunity, making communications teams exponentially more effective, particularly across three core dimensions: volume of output, customization of output, and speed of development and dissemination.

Beyond these core capabilities, AI enables sophisticated early warning systems through real-time monitoring across platforms, generates professional multimedia content without traditional design resources, and provides deep stakeholder intelligence that helps predict reactions before messages go public.

The Modern Communications Team: Building the Stakeholder-First Structure

For decades, we've been reorganizing communications teams around the wrong variables. First, we split everyone into internal and external teams, as if stakeholders cared about our org chart. Then we tried topic-aligned teams where everyone did both internal and external work, which just meant everyone was mediocre at everything. Next came the Centers of Excellence model—small, centralized groups for media relations, employee communications, branding—supporting product and business comms teams scattered across the company. That worked better, but it still organized around our capabilities instead of stakeholder needs.

The model that works today organizes around who actually matters to your business: policy communications experts, financial communications experts, consumer communications experts, employee communications experts, and technology communications experts. Each division goes deep on understanding their stakeholders—what they care about, where they get information, who influences them, and what will actually change their behavior. These aren't generalists who dabble in everything. They're specialists who know their audiences better than anyone else in your company.

This stakeholder-focused structure only works if you solve the translation problem. That's where AI becomes your connective tissue. You need a technologist on your team—not a communicator who learned some Python, but an actual engineer—whose entire job is building the AI infrastructure that lets your specialists focus on influence instead of execution.

This person builds your communications-specific AI environment: a system trained on your company's voice, loaded with your approved language, and programmed with your brand guidelines. They create crisis models pre-loaded with core scenarios, so when something breaks, your team isn't starting from scratch. They develop prompt templates for everything from media pitches to CEO messages to investor talking points. Your policy communications expert provides the strategic insight; AI handles the translation across channels and stakeholders.

Most powerfully, they build synthetic personas—AI-powered simulations of your key stakeholders—that provide instant feedback on plans and messaging. Your financial comms expert tests messages against synthetic personas representing top institutional investors before going public. Your employee comms expert runs restructuring announcements through personas representing different employee segments. This isn't replacing research; it's accelerating iteration so your specialists can pressure-test twenty versions of a message in the time it used to take to craft two.

This infrastructure fundamentally changes your headcount strategy. AI handles the research, analysis, and operations tasks you previously reserved headcount for: monitoring sentiment, analyzing stakeholder conversations, drafting routine communications, customizing messages for different audiences. That frees budget to shift resources toward your technologist and reallocate headcount toward deeper stakeholder specialists. Instead of ten generalists who kind of understand everything, you have six specialists who truly understand their stakeholders plus the AI technologist and infrastructure that lets those six people do the work of twelve.

External agencies still have a role, but it shifts. They should continue to drive the branding and creative work and campaigns that require fresh perspective and specialized creative talent. But more critically, they should be your problem solvers and predictors: experienced counselors who help you stay ahead of knowable issues and navigate the ones you weren't prepared for. A few arms and legs when you need execution support, but mostly strategic guidance from people who've seen your challenges before.

Your internal team focuses on reputation management and stakeholder influence. They're the ones who understand what your investors actually care about when your stock drops, what regulators are really asking for when they send an inquiry, what employees need to hear when you're making difficult decisions. That stakeholder intelligence can't be outsourced.

The companies that master this first will operate at a speed and precision their competitors can't match. While others are still organizing around internal convenience or legacy structures, you'll have built a machine optimized for the only thing that matters: moving the specific people who determine whether your company succeeds or fails.

What Seamless Human–AI Collaboration Looks Like

Teams need to stop viewing AI as a tool and start treating it as an integrated team capability. Here's what that looks like in practice:

- **Human-in-the-loop decision-making** keeps strategic judgment where it belongs while accelerating execution. As Stark emphasizes, "If you're talking about an issue in a crisis, it should be a human. One hundred percent." AI generates options and accelerates research, but humans make final calls on messaging, spokesperson selection, and strategic direction.
- **Integrated workflow design** connects multiple AI capabilities. Advanced implementations use one AI system to draft initial statements, then route that output through another AI trained on executive voice and messaging history to ensure authenticity. The result is both speed and consistency at scale.
- **Boundary discipline** maintains clear limits on AI deployment. Leading organizations never use AI avatars for crisis communications, never rely solely on AI for culturally sensitive messaging, and never substitute AI for authentic human stakeholder engagement.

The competitive advantage goes to organizations that use AI to amplify human judgment and values, not replace them. They deploy these capabilities to become more responsive to stakeholder needs while maintaining the authenticity that makes their communications credible.

YOUR MANTRA IS YOUR STRUCTURE (FIGURE OUT WHERE YOU STAND AND STAND THERE)

The companies that thrive in crises share one characteristic: clarity. Not just clarity of message but clarity of purpose. They know what they stand for, they've organized themselves around those principles, and they're prepared to defend them under pressure.

This clarity isn't just a communications asset; it's an operating principle. It influences who you hire, how you structure teams, what decisions you delegate, and how you measure success. When your stakeholders can tell what you stand for, they know what to expect from you. When they know what to expect, they're more likely to trust you when things go wrong.

Boeing's transformation after the 737 MAX crisis wasn't just about changing messages—it was about reorganizing the entire company around stakeholder trust as an operating principle. We didn't just create new protocols; we rebuilt how the company made decisions about what to say, who should say it, and how quickly we could move.

The specific structures vary wildly across industries. Some companies fuse government relations with legal. Others merge communications with marketing. Still others integrate communications with HR. But strip away the org chart differences, and the highest-performing crisis-ready organizations share three nonnegotiable characteristics.

First, they've wired their operations so internal and external messages move in perfect sync. Employees hear the same story as customers, investors, and regulators—just tailored for relevance. When these companies speak, every voice reinforces the others instead of contradicting them.

Second, they've empowered communicators to make decisions without endless approval loops. When crisis hits, their communications leaders can act with the same authority as any C-suite executive because they've earned that authority through demonstrated judgment.

Third, and most fundamentally, they've organized themselves around stakeholder needs rather than internal convenience. They didn't ask, "What structure is easiest for us?" They asked, "What structure serves the people who determine whether we survive?" Then they built that, even when it was uncomfortable.

The specific structures vary: Some companies combine government relations with legal, others have comms with marketing, and others put comms with HR. But the underlying commitment is consistent: They've organized themselves around stakeholder needs rather than internal convenience.

Structure to Enhance Messaging Speed and Dexterity

Relatedly, they've also structured themselves around message-to-market imperatives. The velocity of modern communications demands organizational structures that can operate at campaign speed. Robert Gibbs, who now serves as chief communications and public affairs officer for Warner Bros. Discovery, draws directly from his political experience to explain what this looks like:

> It feels like a campaign. You need somebody who, every minute of every day, is scanning to figure out: what are your opportunities and what do you have to position against. You need people in lanes they understand, and that means having the dexterity to hop around really quickly.

This isn't just about crisis response; it's about daily operational reality. Political campaigns succeed because they combine constant vigilance with rapid response capabilities. They don't wait for scheduled meetings to react to developments. They don't require extensive approval processes to pivot strategy.

Gibbs points to a specific example: "We have this great team in marketing at HBO Max that just tries to look for viral moments of things that are happening on shows, but also in society that we can pair off of. You've got to be thinking about how to own your own narrative more."

This "viral moment hunting" represents a fundamental shift from reactive to proactive communications. Instead of waiting for others to set the narrative, you're constantly looking for opportunities to insert your voice into ongoing conversations.

The takeaway isn't that you should copy Visa's people model or Moderna's startup approach. The takeaway is that you should learn from them: Understand why those companies made the choices they did, evaluate how those choices might apply to your stakeholder landscape, and design accordingly.

Key Learnings:

Start with your stakeholders. Build your structure around their needs. Align your operating system with your values. Enhance your capabilities with AI where it amplifies human judgment. In a crisis, you will be tested on all four elements. If you're built for it, you'll bend but not break. If you're not, the crisis will reveal exactly where your weaknesses lie.

CHAPTER FOURTEEN

COMMS AT THE CENTER OF THE STORM

It was July 2017, and the gleaming Pratt & Whitney GTF engine sat like a monument to American ingenuity outside of the Rayburn House Office Building, just steps from the US Capitol. Congress members wandered among the displays, running their hands along the precision-engineered components. Media clustered around the engine, cameras capturing every angle of this technological marvel that represented the future of sustainable aviation.

My team had orchestrated every detail. We'd brought in suppliers and workers from across the country—the people who'd actually built this revolutionary engine that would power the next generation of aircraft. The timing wasn't coincidental. We'd positioned this showcase directly adjacent to Trump's Made in America Week, and I'd coined the perfect label for the press: "An engine for the US economy."

We flew in small suppliers, corralled members from nearly forty different congressional offices to learn from frontline workers about the moving truck–sized engine, and arranged for company leadership to explain the program's local impact on their respective states. We'd taken pictures of members of Congress from both parties standing with our workers next to the engine and sent them to news outlets in the members' local districts, accompanied by stats on job impact to give them all a little boost of positive coverage back home.

It should have been a clean win: pure positive press for Pratt & Whitney's innovation and American manufacturing.

But shadows loomed over our perfect moment. One year earlier, UTC had struck a celebrated deal with President Trump to save jobs at Carrier in Indiana. Now, twelve months later, that agreement was generating renewed scrutiny. When the first set of layoffs in line with the plan was announced in June of 2017, reporters looking to make the Carrier decision a referendum on Trump's dealmaking abilities wrote a wave of stories criticizing the layoffs and declaring that Trump had failed to prevent the job losses despite all of his proclamations.

The president, so incensed by the negative press, called our CEO, Greg Hayes, the day after the stories hit and aggressively demanded that he reverse the company's position and keep the jobs in the US. Greg reminded him that the reductions were in keeping with the terms of their agreement. As the one-year anniversary of the original Carrier deal inched closer, the media were asking more and more pointed questions about the status of the Indiana jobs.

WHY DON'T *YOU* COMMUNICATE?

Bob Leduc, president of Pratt & Whitney, had agreed to participate in the Capitol Hill showcase. UTC's chief communications and government relations officers—my two direct bosses—and I had pushed for the showcase to happen in DC, hoping to shift the Carrier narrative.

Bob understood the value of good press, but he'd made his position clear from the start. This was about the engine business and American manufacturing excellence. When my communications team briefed him on how to handle questions raised about Carrier, our sister company, his frustration simmered just below the surface.

The event was unfolding beautifully. The congressional members were genuinely impressed by the technology. Suppliers were telling their stories with pride. The media coverage was shaping up exactly as we'd hoped, until a communications executive asked Bob to step away from a meeting with suppliers to do an interview. That's when Bob absolutely lost it.

"I don't understand why I have to be the one talking to the press," he exploded. "You're communications. Why don't *you* communicate?"

In that moment of raw frustration, Bob had crystallized his two deepest concerns. First, he did not want his good story getting tied up with a bad, unrelated story when his should have been a clean win. Second, he had a business to run and didn't feel like it should be his responsibility to play cleanup for a part of the company that wasn't his. Why wouldn't the team charged with communications handle that?

That moment reinforced something critical: Business executives are there to run the business. Communication is part of effective management, but it's not what they wake up thinking about or want to think about. The communicators of the future won't just script talking points and coach executives; they'll step up and be the voice of the company when needed, especially in the tough moments. That's what a White House

The communicators of the future won't just script talking points and coach executives; they'll step up and be the voice of the company when needed, especially in the tough moments.

press secretary does for a political administration. Why shouldn't a CCO do the same for a business?

PUTTING COMMS FRONT AND CENTER

Too often, communicators put themselves in a behind-the-scenes box, a self-imposed prison of sorts. Executives don't necessarily expect us to stay there, but we've convinced ourselves that it's where we belong. If anything, top executives want us to share the burden of being front and center. Breaking the mindset that communication belongs behind the scenes isn't just freeing; it strengthens the entire business. Political communicators already operate this way. They do more than just advise elected officials; they own the message and deliver it themselves when the stakes are highest.

Communicators need to be equipped not only to direct communication but also to own it. Bob wasn't being difficult. He was being honest about what the job now requires. Business leaders need communications professionals who function as strategic counselors—leaders who can take the heat, control the narrative, and represent the company's interests with the same authority as any C-suite executive.

That moment on Capitol Hill taught me that we're not just behind-the-scenes advisors anymore. We're frontline leaders. And if we're not ready to step into that role, someone else will—or worse, no one will, and the narrative will get away from us entirely.

The world had changed. Were we ready to change with it?

WHEN COMPANIES GET IT RIGHT: WHAT FIRST MOVERS GAIN

While competitors stumble through crises, companies that master certain principles control their destinies. Take Eli Lilly's response to the November 2022 fake Twitter crisis that initially wiped $15 billion from its market cap. When a verified imposter account tweeted, "insulin is free now," the company didn't just defend or deflect. Within months, it transformed the narrative completely by announcing a real $35 insulin price cap in March 2023.[80] It turned a crisis into credibility, converting public anger into brand goodwill. The fake tweet became a catalyst for real action that the company's stakeholders had been demanding for years.

Or consider Johnson & Johnson's legendary 1982 Tylenol response, which created the playbook that every business school still teaches.[81] When seven people died from cyanide-laced capsules, Johnson & Johnson didn't hesitate, hedge, or calculate. Within hours, it recalled thirty-one million bottles worth $100 million, stopped all production and advertising, and worked openly with law enforcement. CEO James Burke personally appeared on national TV to explain their actions. The result? Within a year, Tylenol regained its entire market share and established Johnson & Johnson as the gold standard for crisis management. The company's willingness to act decisively on its values—putting people before profit—became its competitive advantage.

---

80 Graig Graziosi, "'Hero' Journalist Congratulated After Eli Lilly Lowers Price of Insulin After His Spoof Tweet Raised Awareness," *Independent*, March 2, 2023, https://www.independent.co.uk/news/world/americas/journalist-eli-lilly-insulin-prices-b2293168.html.

81 Jennifer Latson, "How Poisoned Tylenol Became a Crisis-Management Teaching Model," *TIME*, September 29, 2014, https://time.com/3423136/tylenol-deaths-1982/.

These companies understood something fundamental: In a velocity economy, first movers don't just survive crises; they use them to separate themselves from competitors. While others scramble to respond, leaders shape the response. While others defend their old positions, leaders define new standards. While others lose control of their narratives, leaders write the endings to their own stories.

WHAT WE'VE LEARNED: THE CRITICAL POINTS THAT DEFINE WINNERS

Speed over perfection in the velocity economy: Today's environment punishes deliberation more than imperfection. The NFL's response to Damar Hamlin's cardiac arrest showed the new standard: immediate, transparent communication even without complete information. Companies that respond in hours control their narrative; those that wait become victims of someone else's storytelling.

Audience segmentation in the era of micro-tribes: Mass communication is dead. Each stakeholder group requires different messengers, channels, and frames. UTC had to speak simultaneously to political allies, business critics, union members, and shareholders during the Carrier crisis, all with different expectations and emotional investments.

Data-driven impact over vanity metrics: Move beyond reach and impressions to persuasion and behavior change. Metrics such as share of voice, message pull-through, and sentiment have real business implications. Are policymakers repeating your messages? Are influencers citing your company as "getting it right"?

Human authenticity in an AI-saturated world: The safety executive's breakdown during the media training with Gibbs and me became the most credible statement anyone had heard from company leadership.

In an era of corporate speak and algorithmic content, genuine human emotion makes you more credible, not less.

The one constant—values-driven conviction: While everything changes about our field, one thing never will: People want to understand where you stand, and they need to believe you'll stand there. Have conviction. Live your values consistently. The companies that win in the long term are those whose actions align with their stated principles, even when it costs them. *Especially when it costs them.*

THE EVOLUTION OF THE COMMUNICATOR: FROM SUPPORT FUNCTION TO STRATEGIC LEADER

While the chief impact officer title may have fallen out of favor in the past few years, the rising influence of the communications professional as a strategic leader continues as smart companies continue to consolidate communications, government relations, and corporate purpose under unified leadership. Here are some examples:

- **Tara DiJulio at GE Aerospace** was elevated from CCO to chief corporate affairs officer in 2024 and oversees communications, government relations, and brand strategy.
- **Dani Dudeck at Instacart** was tapped to serve as the company's chief corporate affairs officer, managing communications, government affairs, and social impact initiatives.
- **Stephen Kehoe at PepsiCo** combined communications, government affairs, and public policy under one umbrella.
- **Jill Hazelbaker at Uber** has long led a global team that integrates marketing, communications, and public policy.

Forward-thinking companies are already following the White House press secretary model, whereby communicators own the message and deliver it themselves when the stakes are at their highest.

YOUR NINETY-DAY TRANSFORMATION ROAD MAP

Revamping a corporate crisis communications infrastructure doesn't happen overnight. It happens in stages: assessing where you are, building up new systems, and then integrating and executing. I offer a sample twelve-week road map as a guide through this transformation.

Weeks 1 to 2: Audit Your Current State

- Test your crisis response time. Can you respond with substance to any major story in under two hours?
- Map your real influencer ecosystem. Who actually moves opinion in your industry, beyond traditional media?
- Identify your top three narrative vulnerabilities and assign direct accountability for each.

Weeks 3 to 6: Start Building Infrastructure

- Create appropriate direct-to-audience channels that bypass traditional gatekeepers.
- Establish a unified reputation council with regular standing meetings across functions.
- Develop scenario-planning protocols and integrate them into strategic reviews.

Weeks 7 to 12: Consolidate, Execute, and Integrate

- Consider consolidating communications, government affairs, and corporate purpose functions under unified strategic leadership.
- Implement new metrics focused on persuasion and behavior change, not just reach.
- Train your team to step forward as voices of the company, not just behind-the-scenes advisors.

Remember, every organization has a different culture, setup, and orbit of stakeholders. Any changes need to be responsive to your lived reality.

THE FOUR FUTURE IMPERATIVES: WHAT'S COMING NEXT

As communicator roles and the environment we operate in evolve, we'll see the following with greater frequency:

- **Targeting will move from segmentation to hyper-personalization**. Instead of targeting "manufacturing workers," we'll be reaching "third-shift Boeing assembly workers in Everett concerned about job security." The technology to go granular with targeting exists; the strategic discipline doesn't yet.
- **Leadership's coordination with communications will evolve into integration, with communicators taking on leadership roles**. As the future unfolds, organizations will need to find ways to truly and legitimately integrate leadership around all things reputation and society, offering the CEO and board a single counselor to turn to for guidance.

The question is whether communicators will be positioned to occupy that role.

- **Focus will move from feel-good reach to ruthless impact.** In tomorrow's comms world, we will need to be ruthless about pouring our resources into the things that create impact and dropping the things that don't. No more vanity metrics. No more activities that feel good but change nothing.
- **We'll go from treating AI like a tool to embracing it as a teammate.** To thrive in an AI-driven future, we will need to view AI not only as a tool but as a core part of our team. We need to embrace AI as a partner in elevating our function and driving strong, more nuanced, and more resilient outcomes for our companies and organizations.

SOURCES OF HOPE: WHY THIS MOMENT BELONGS TO COMMUNICATORS

The Democratization of Voice

When then Walmart's Dave Tovar took a red pen to *The New York Times* op-ed piece,[82] he showed how companies can boldly reclaim their own narrative. Direct-to-audience platforms give communicators unprecedented power to reach stakeholders without intermediaries.

- **The premium on truth-telling**: In an age of deepfakes and disinformation, authentic human communication becomes more valuable. The NFL's Damar Hamlin response proved

82 Diana Bradley, "How Walmart Decided to Take a Red Pen to a *New York Times* Op-Ed," *PRWeek*, June 25, 2014, https://www.prweek.com/article/1300484/walmart-decided-red-pen-new-york-times-op-ed.

that transparency about uncertainty builds credibility rather than undermining it.

- **The integration opportunity**: As boundaries blur between communications, government affairs, and ESG, communicators can become the strategic hub. We understand narrative, stakeholders, and timing better than other functions.
- **The human advantage**: AI can analyze sentiment, but it can't build authentic relationships. Our humanity becomes our competitive advantage.

THE CHOICE: LEAD OR BE LED

As we take on new and greater leadership responsibilities, we as communications professionals will need to hone our skills. The comms leaders of the future will need to bring:

- Policy fluency and a deeper understanding of political influence
- Media specialization across tech, financial, and consumer ecosystems
- Metrics discipline focused on reputation health indicators
- Cultural intelligence across diverse stakeholder environments
- AI and data fluency in service of the business

Taking on a greater leadership role requires courage. It means taking ownership instead of deflecting responsibility, speaking truth to power when messages are unpopular, and stepping into the light when executives need us to be the shield.

THE NEW RULES FOR STRATEGIC LEADERS

I was a teenager when I learned that survival isn't about avoiding danger; it's about knowing what to do when danger finds you. That lesson has served me in every crisis I've managed since.

The communications professionals who will lead in the next decade aren't the ones with the most polished talking points. They're the ones who understand that this job is about scenario planning, not spin. They're the ones willing to walk into the mess instead of waiting for someone else to clean it up.

If you're ready to do this work, here's what it requires:

- **Own your voice.** Stop waiting for permission to communicate. Build direct channels to your stakeholders. If you're still running every statement through three layers of approval, you're already too slow.
- **Integrate your function.** Communications isn't separate from government relations, corporate purpose, or business strategy. Position yourself as the counselor who understands how all these pieces connect or watch someone else take that seat.
- **Measure what matters.** Awareness is bullshit. Reach is vanity. The only metrics that matter are persuasion and behavior change. If you can't show that your work moved someone to think or act differently, you're just making noise.
- **Live your values.** Hypocrisy will destroy you faster than any activist campaign. If your actions don't match your stated principles, you have no foundation for anything else. Consistency isn't a nice-to-have—it's the whole game.
- **Embrace the mess.** Nothing about this work is clean. You're going to wade into situations where there are no good options, only less-bad ones. You're going to make calls at 2:00 a.m. with

incomplete information. Get comfortable with ambiguity or find another profession.

The scenario planning that kept me alive in dangerous situations growing up—understanding your environment, assessing threats, having contingency plans—is the same capability keeping companies alive in dangerous narrative environments. Both require constant vigilance, pattern recognition, and the ability to move fast when the situation changes.

Here's what's actually at stake:

Corporations lose their social license to operate when they can't navigate the political minefield we're living in. Democracy breaks down when lies travel faster than truth and no one knows who to trust. Industries lose competitive advantage when reputation damage becomes a weekly occurrence instead of a rare crisis.

The companies dominating the next decade are being built right now by leaders who understand that communication isn't a support function—it's core infrastructure. While your competitors are still debating whether to invest in these capabilities, you need to be shaping markets, influencing policy, and controlling narratives.

For those willing to evolve, the tools are more powerful than they've ever been. The need is greater than it's ever been. But the window won't stay open forever.

So here's my final piece of advice: The threats aren't theoretical. They're not coming someday. They're here. Your competitors are getting better at this while you read this sentence. Your employees are watching to see if you mean what you say. Your customers are one TikTok away from deciding you're the villain in someone else's story.

You hope reality doesn't find you, or you can build the capacity to handle that reality when it arrives. The choice is up to you.

Don't get caught slippin'.